Have Better Memory

Your Memory How It Works and How to Improve It

Ivan Harmon

Book 1

Boost Your Brain Power

Learn Better, Smarter, and faster - Scientifically Proven Guides to Sharpen Your Focus and Retrain Your Brain

Ivan Harmon

Copyright 2017 by Ivan Harmon - All rights reserved.

The following book is reproduced with the goal of providing information that is as accurate and reliable as possible. Regardless, purchasing this ebook can be seen as consent to the fact that both the publisher and the author of this book are in no way experts on the topics discussed within and that any recommendations or suggestions that are made herein are for entertainment purposes only. Professionals should be consulted as needed prior to undertaking any of the action endorsed herein.

This declaration is deemed fair and valid by both the American Bar Association and the Committee of Publishers Association and is legally binding throughout the United States.

Furthermore, the transmission, duplication or reproduction of any of the following work including specific information will be considered an illegal act irrespective of if it is done electronically or in print. This extends to creating a secondary or tertiary copy of the work or a recorded copy and is only allowed with express written consent from the Publisher. All additional rights reserved.

The information in the following pages is broadly considered to be a truthful and accurate account of facts and as such any inattention, use or misuse of the information in question by the reader will render any resulting actions solely under their purview. There are no scenarios in which the publisher or the original author of this work can be in any fashion deemed liable for any hardship or damages that may befall them after undertaking information described herein.

Additionally, the information in the following pages is intended only for informational purposes and should thus be thought of as universal. As befitting its nature, it is presented without assurance regarding its prolonged validity or interim quality. Trademarks that are mentioned are done without written consent and can in no way be considered an endorsement from the trademark holder.

Table of contents

INTRODUCTION 1

CHAPTER 1: THE ESSENCE OF MEMORY 3

CHAPTER 2: PROBLEM-SOLVING 13

CHAPTER 3: THOUGHT 23

CHAPTER 4: LEARNING 49

CHAPTER 5: ATTENTION SPAN 53

CHAPTER 6: ANOTHER RELATABLE INSPIRATION - THOMAS EDISON 83

CONCLUSION 129

Introduction

Thank you for purchasing this book. In it, you will find all of the information you are looking for to increase your mental functioning. If you find you have problems with focusing, problem solving, or remembering things, this is the book for you. Backed by scientific discoveries, and based on the way your brain works, these tips will help you get to the root of the problem in no time.

If you feel like this book may just be words on a page, fear not. This book has relatable instances from famous people, including one you would have never even suspected had any problems mentally functioning at all.

I hope you enjoy this book and thank you again for your purchase.

Chapter 1: The Essence of Memory

Memory is the space in the mind where information is stored, and used from there. It can be encoded and decoded all from the one area of the brain that controls it.

Think of it as an information processing system where there are two sections. Long and short term memory. The short term memory releases information that is not deemed necessary beyond a short amount of time, and the long-term memory stores information that are seen as important by your brain. For example, if you are not going to see a person ever again, you will only need to know their name for the duration of the conversation you are having with them, and then you don't need to remember it any further. This would use your short term memory. However, if you work with someone every day, you would need to know their name for a long amount of time. Therefore, you would commit their name to your long-term memory.

There are two systems of memory. Explicit and implicit, or declarative and nondeclarative. Designed for memory storage and retrieval, these two systems work through your brain depending on the signals that are sent to them. Declarative, or explicit memory is the act of recalling information or consciously storing memory, such as a phone number. This requires you to know that you want to remember something.

Nondeclarative memory, also known as Implicit memory, is an unconscious act. Your brain stores things that you need to remember without you even knowing that it does. Such as the features of a specific character. Memories of a really fun day where you just lost yourself in the activities you were doing with no thought about thinking of it in the future, even though you will fondly look back on that and smile.

Memory is not perfect. There are many different factors that can affect it, such as the amount of importance you see something and the amount of attention you give different stimuli when attempting to remember something. Damage to your hippocampus, which controls the memory process, can also affect what you can remember. Your long-term memory may fade over time if a memory has not been called upon in a while. Just as an old photograph fades, so do memories. You may find yourself forgetting how a loved one's voice sounds when they have been gone for a long time, for example.

There are three main stages to retrieving and forming a memory:

- Encoding: which is a registration process. You register the memory and prepare to store it.
- Storage: Your brain stores the encoded information in both the short and long-term memory.
- Retrieval: This is where you call the memory back from where it is stored. You do this using a cue, or part of the memory, such as a date.

If you struggle with the loss of memory, you may suffer from forgetfulness. If you cannot remember things at all, you may be suffering from amnesia.

Sensory memory

This is where you can see something for a very short amount of time, and remember it clearly for a little bit of time after seeing the object. However, the more stimuli there is in the picture, the less that a person can remember, as the brain feels overwhelmed. Some people can handle more stimuli than others depending on how their brain functions. This process is involuntary, and while there are things you can do to improve your sensory memory if you do not have it, there is not much that can be done about it.

There are three types of sensory memory. Iconic, echoic, and haptic. Iconic is rapidly decaying memories that deal with visual stimuli. Echoic have to do with auditory stimuli, and haptic refers to stimuli through the touch or taste sensation.

Short-term memory

Also referred to as primary memory, this is the part of your memory that has to do with the here-and-now sort of circumstances. In the introduction to this chapter, we went over how if you were not going to see someone again, their name would only be found in your short-term memory, and then it would decay over time. This is okay because you have no need for that memory.

Short-term memory relies more on auditory stimuli than visual stimuli to store the memories. Studies have shown that people who heard the information remembered it for a longer amount of time than if they took the information visually.[1]

Long-Term Memory

Long-Term Mermory is immeasurable in the amount of time that it can store information. Some people can remember things for their entire life, and some people lose information after a few years, making it hard to measure how long the long-term memory stays intact. Scientist speculates it has to do with the integrity of the hippocampus.

---

[1] http://www.csl.georgetown.edu/publications/Koo%20et%20al.,%202008%20NYAS.pdf

Long-term memory is recorded episodically and semantically, unlike the auditory fashion in which the short-term memory is recorded. This means that people may have a hard time remembering sounds over time, but they can remember things they have seen and patterns they have noticed. Long-term memory is a bit of a mystery even to this day on how it works exactly because everyone remembers things differently.

Science has suggested that long-term memory has to do with DNA and may be hard to change the capacity and things that you could remember through exercises.

Working memory

Working memory is when your memory is constantly working on a loop. This can be caused by many things, and often times it is very useful, such as when you are working and have to remember the tasks you still need to do. Also when performing a task, you are using your working memory. However, some scientists speculate that your working memory is also responsible for PTSD (Post Traumatic Stress

Disorder) and nightmares. There is no solid link yet, but it is in the works.

When you tie your shoes, you are using your working memory. When you type a document, you are using your working memory. Everything you do that you had to learn how to do, you are using your working memory.

Genetics

While the studies are still fairly new, there is some suggestion that genetics play a major role in your memory skills. There are more studies being done every year. Here are some of the discoveries that have been made so far.

In infancy

Until about thirty years ago, it was believed that infants could not use any of the sequences of memory. It was believed that memory was not established until around a year of age, and it was shaky at best then. However, since then, it has been established that babies' memories begin working from the time they are born. Such as how a newborn recognizes their mother's voice from her speaking while the baby was in the womb. As the baby grows, their memory skills expand.

By around six months of age, a baby can remember colors or patterns and sounds in their short-term memory and can remember how to make a sound from a toy, or how to roll over. Little things, but it shows that they do have the beginnings of memory. By nine months, a baby can recall a two-step process. This was an even bigger discovery, as babies were thought to not be able to do that until they were two years of age or older up until that point.

However, baby memory is not very strong, and they forget things often. It takes a lot of repetition to help them continue to remember, suggesting that their long-term memories are not fully formed at this point. This is called Infantile Amnesia.

Aging

It is no secret that we fear aging for fear of losing our memories. Some elderly people even forget their own children, and how to take care of themselves. This is known as Alzheimer's disease. It is a form of rapidly progressing amnesia that affects a lot of seniors from all walks of life. Younger people can be affected by it as well, but it is more likely that it happens in the senior years. While not everyone is affected by amnesia, most seniors will find that they do have some sort of memory recollection issues. This causes the belief that long-term memory degrades over time.

Effects of physical exercise

Physical exercise is extremely important when it comes to maintaining a healthy memory. Science has found that people who stay active have easier times remembering important information over long periods of time. This could be because your brain is getting more blood flow when you are active, but it could also be attributed to the fact that you think about things when you are working out.

Influencing factors

The most influencing factor on your memory is interference. Whether it be personal or auxiliary interference, it will still cause issues with your memory, because the external or even internal stimuli diverts your focus, and splits the signals, so you have a harder time memorizing things.

Stress can affect your memory the most. When you are stressed, your brain is more focused on what is bothering you and trying to keep you calm. You may find that recalling memories when stressed is almost impossible, or that remembering anything can be difficult which can add more stress to your life.

Sleep also affects your memory. Not getting enough sleep is enough to significantly decrease your ability to memorize anything, or to accurately recall previous memories.

Chapter 2: Problem-solving

If you are like a lot of people, problem-solving is not your forte. It can be difficult to find yourself in a hard situation, because you may struggle to find a way out. A lot of people have a problem processing enough information to solve a problem quickly, and if you are one of those people, you are not alone.

You may be wondering what this has to do with your memory, and the truth is, they tie in together very well. You have to have a good memory to remember things that will help you solve a problem at hand. Also, having good problem-solving skills can help improve your memory, because some situations may seem relevant, and you will subconsciously store it to your memory.

Definition

There are many different definitions of problems solving. However, the one we will use here is the one that refers to human problem-solving, rather than computerized problem-solving. Problem-solving is the act of figuring out a solution to a difficult situation by determining a multiple step process to defeat the obstacle.

Problem-solving strategies

Problem-solving is viewed as a cycle. You define the problem, brainstorm a solution, test the solution, adjust for errors, and then solve the problem. Only to have to start all over again when a new problem arises. We do this every day in minor ways, such as deciding what to where, finding a detour around construction on our way to work, and thinking about what to have for dinner.

The system of solving a problem is much like the scientific method. You have to identify the problem, hypothesize a solution, test it, fix it, and present the solution. This makes it

Chapter 2: Problem-solving

easier to determine the next step of problem-solving if you are not sure where to go.

There are two forms of problem-solving. One is solving a problem with only one solution, such as a math problem. The other is a little more difficult because it is solving a problem with multiple solutions, or solutions that are always changing, such as what you should get your coworker for their birthday. So to solve problems, you need some techniques to solve them. See below for some ideas.

- Abstraction: Using a model before applying into the real system.
- Analogy: Explaining and clarifying through a comparison of two things.
- Brainstorming: Arriving to a solution through combining and developing ideas and large number of solutions.
- Divide and Conquer: Simplifying complex problems to make it easier to solve.
- Hypothesis Testing: Proving assumptions using the tested data and gathered information.

- Lateral Thinking: Solving problems through creative and indirect approach.
- Means-end Analysis: Step-by-step choosing of actions towards the goal.
- Method of Focal Objects: Combining totally different objects to make something new.
- Morphological Analysis: An ordered way of solving non-quantified problems.
- Proof: Proving unsolvable problems. The starting point in solving the problem is where the proof failed.
- Reduction: Changing a problem to another problem to come up with solutions.
- Research: Solving the problem using the existing solutions.
- Root Cause Analysis: Finding out what causes the problem.
- Trial and Error: Using various solutions until finally solving the problem.

Barriers

There are reasons that problem-solving is viewed as difficult. This is because there are often barriers to solving a problem. If it were easy, it would not be called *problem*-solving, so of course, there are going to be some difficulties. Being able to define what these barriers could be can help you out exponentially because you will know what to look for when problem-solving.

Confirmation bias

Biases will get you in trouble, and they are no less dangerous in problem-solving. It is important that you go into solving the problem without a preconceived notion of the outcome. When you are going to solve a problem, you may have an idea of what will work. This can lead you to be stubborn and unwilling to change or adapt when it doesn't work. This is known as confirmation bias.

Mental set

Mindset is the biggest portion of problems for your problem-solving skills. Many people feel that their way is the only way and that there is no other way to do what they are doing. Scientists have noted that when they give a set of people a test, and they figured out the solution to the problem, that is the way they would prefer to do similar tests in the future, even if presented with a simpler solution.

If you are stuck in the mindset that the way you know is the only way, then you will generally pass over a simpler, more effective solution in lieu of the way you know. This can cause problems when you are problem-solving because you are stuck with your own mindset that you know what is best.

How to Improve Your Problem-solving Skills

1. Dance Your Heart Out

Dancing has a positive impact on your brain. It can help with your problem-solving skills because you have to plan out each step that you take. If you make a misstep, then you have to quickly figure out how to recover. The physical exercise is good for your brain as well, as it helps improve cognitive function. When you are dancing, you are improving your problem-solving skills, so get out there, and dance like no one is watching.

2. Work out Your Brain with Logic Puzzles or Games

Logic games are great at helping you develop problem-solving skills, due to their need for a cause and effect sort of mindset. Playing chess is a great way to improve your problem-solving skills because you constantly have to adjust your strategy to the other player's moves. You want to come out on top, so you come up with not one, but a variety of solutions for each move and choose the best one. Games like chess are great for improving your cognitive function.

3. Get a Good Night's Sleep

Sleep. It is such a wonderful word. However, sometimes it can be hard to attain. Especially if you have a big problem to face. However, staying up all night agonizing over it is not the way to work through the problem. You have to make sure that you are not losing sleep over your problems. Sleep will refresh your brain, and allow you to have a clear head when you are going to tackle the problem.

4. Work out to Some Tunes

While exercise will help you think more clearly, and get the blood flowing to your brain, it does not necessarily help the problem-solving skills. However, when you add music to the mix like you would with dancing, you add another thing is going on in the background of your mind which forces you to focus more. Music helps you increase your problem-solving skills pretty well.

5. Keep an "Idea Journal" with You

Journals are a great way to keep your mind cleared. You can get your thoughts out as soon as they cross your mind. This helps keep yourself organized, and you don't have to worry about forgetting anything because you are keeping track of your important thoughts.

6. Participate in Yoga

Yoga may seem like a strange way to help with problem-solving and improving your ability to do so, but the intense awareness of your body movements and your breathing leaves you figuring out the best way to execute a move and be able to hold it without much strain. This will help you improve your problem-solving skills tenfold.

7. Eat Some Cheerios (And Then Think About It)

Cheerios are more than just heart health. Eating them is a great way to improve your problem-solving skills, as you are forced to figure out why the last few cheerios run away from your spoon, and the best way to scoop them up without slurping them out of the bowl along with the milk.

8. Use Mind Maps to Help Visualize the Problem

Not a map like a road map, a mental map. These can be things such as a flow chart or a Venn diagram. These will help you organize your thoughts and visualize a solution to your problem.

9. Create "Psychological Distance"

Don't get so caught up in your ideas that you refuse to see the best solution to the problem. This means that you must mentally separate yourself from the problem, and look at it from an unbiased and objective point of view. You may even get someone else's input on the problem. This will help you with improving your problem-solving skills by teaching you to be objective.

10. Play Some Soccer

Soccer is amazing for problem-solving skills, because you have to coordinate your feet with a ball, and you cannot use your hands. Not using your hands presents a problem, because most sports require the use of hands. When you are playing soccer, you are constantly problem-solving on the field, trying to figure out how to get the ball in the goal without using your hands.

Chapter 3: Thought

There is no solid definition of thought because it is something that is viewed as abstract. This means that there is no way to truly define it. However, it is thought to be the collection of ideas that lead to thinking.

It is important to know more about thought to understand how it works in order to be successful at keeping your train of thought, which we will go over in the next chapter.

Thinking allows us to process information that has been given to us. It allows us to figure things out, and understand the world around us. There is no telling what all goes into thought, but there are some ideas.

Psychology

It is believed that thought is designed to help humans figure out what is going on around them. Humans are believed to be the only species that actively think about what they are doing, rather than acting on instinct. It is a psychological mechanism to help protect humans from injuring themselves through their instincts. It is also believed that having the ability to think is what has led humans to be on top of the food chain.

However, some people have trouble with thinking. They may find that their mind is clouded and that there is no way around it. You can improve your thinking skills exponentially using these few tips.

To improve your thinking, you have to improve your self-discipline, because thought and self-discipline are directly linked. If you can improve your self-discipline, you will be better at controlling your train of thought so that you can stay on track. When you can control your train of thought, you will have a stronger attention span, which we will get into later, and you will be able to problem-solve better. It will also help your memory as well because you will not get sidetracked trying to remember something or trying to recall a memory.

Self-Discipline

Self-discipline. You have probably heard the term more times than you can count. Or maybe you heard it called will power. Either way, it is a term that is tossed around quite a bit. Have you given any thought to what it means? Not many people really do, they just feel like they have it innately.

What is self-discipline? The best way to know is to start with the definition and work from there.

Self-discipline is defined as the ability to find a reason to stick with something for a long period of time, even if you may not want to. Especially if you do not want to. However, this rings kind of empty if you think about it. If you do not want to do something, how are you going to find a reason to want to do it? The answer is you. You find the want to within yourself. Maybe it is pride in a job well done, or maybe there is a reward that is waiting on the other end of the job.

Whatever the reason, you have to find a reason to stick with the task at hand.

This doesn't really give much insight into how you can find the willpower to do something though. Sure you could find the want to inside of you, but it has to be there first, and if it is not, then you may have a problem.

You have to build the habits that will give you stronger will power to do the things that you do not want to do. Just like with focusing, it takes practice to get better at disciplining yourself to do what needs to be done. It takes time as well. Gladiators were not made overnight, and you too have to put in the time and effort to really make a difference in your life.

It is not just about the ability to do something; it is about the ability to do something, no matter what the obstacles are. Self-discipline involves a lot of factors, including being able to adapt to situations with ease. Many people, when faced with an obstacle, want to just give up. People with good amounts of self-discipline will just push on and continue moving up the ladder.

It is pertinent to develop a strong sense of self-discipline within yourself that you can truly rely on. If you don't then you may find that you have a hard time getting to where you need to go, from where you have begun. The truth is, people who lack self-discipline often find that they have a harder time achieving their goals, and meeting deadlines because procrastination tends to be their best friend. People with self-discipline are generally viewed as ambitious, and full of drive. These are the people who get their work done early and look for others to help. They are never satisfied with good enough and are always looking for ways to improve themselves.

What it Takes to Develop Self-Discipline

No one is born with innate amounts of self-discipline. We are all born with a need to take care of, rather than a need to take care of others. That is why babies are not born able to walk. You have to develop your self-discipline beyond what you may naturally develop growing up.

Most people need a few things to happen to be able to work on their self-discipline, and that is okay because developing self-discipline in itself takes a form of discipline that not everyone is used to.

Having a Reason WHY!

Why would we develop any sort of self-discipline if we did not have a reason to? We wouldn't. Humans are naturally passive as a form of safeguarding themselves. If there is no reason to be stronger then most people will not go to the gym. The same goes with self-discipline. If there is no reason for you to try to be better than you were if you do not have anything to strive for. We are a culture of motivation and inspiration. If you have a reason to be better than you were, then you will try to reach that goal. Perhaps it's personal gain, or maybe it is something else entirely. You need to determine what you want and why you want it. You also need to find out what are the things that you need complete and how to complete them.

Distinguishing the these things will help be inspired to turn out superior to anything you were.

Having an Unwavering Commitment

Commitment. This is a word that can be enough to make a grown man shudder. However, if you are committed to raising your self-discipline, then you will find that sticking with the program is a lot easier than you would have ever imagined. If you can stick with the same sports team for years despite their massive losing streak, then you can believe in yourself for a few days.

Keeping Yourself Accountable

No one is going to force you to better yourself. You have to make yourself do it. Self-accountability is the hardest thing that a person can do, and it is also one of the best gifts you can give yourself. It is a self-discipline in itself because without self-accountability, you will not be able to reprimand yourself if your willpower slips. No one is going to scold you but you, so you have to hold yourself to a high standard and avoid falling from that.

Having Rewards and Penalties

Do you remember being a kid, and when you did something wrong you got in trouble, but when you did something right you got an award? Well, adult life is like that as well, only you are the one who dishes out the penalties and rewards. The trick is not to reward yourself for a poor job, even though it can be tempting. You have to find a system and stick with it.

Having rewards and penalties will give you more of a reason to hold yourself accountable. You want to get the rewards, and it will make it easier to do what you want to do if you have a reward to look forward to.

You can reward yourself any time you take a step in the right direction towards your goal, however, make sure that the

Chapter 3: Thought

reward matches the size of the step. If you are on a diet, and you have a weekend long cheat binge after dieting for two days, you are nullifying your progress, making it harder to get anywhere. For small steps, think small rewards. For big steps, think big rewards. Of course, penalties should match the offense as well.

Set Standards

You have to set your personal standards for yourself, and there are some questions that will guide you through:

1. What individual measures should I maintain?
2. What are the practices and decisions should I acknowledge and should not?
3. In what manner will I rectify things when I become misguided?

You have to make an agreement with yourself, and treat it like a legally binding contract. This will make it easier to hold yourself accountable. Especially if you stay within your personal means. It is harder to achieve a goal that is set way higher than you could realistically accomplish.

Having a Competitive Environment

Humans get bored fairly easily. They have no mental stimulation or reason to push forward, and it gets harder and harder to continue on towards their goal. The key is to always be in competition. Whether it means keeping your environment competitive or asking a friend to compete with you so that you have a reason to reach your goal, competition keeps things lively and fresh so that it is easier to develop your self-discipline.

If you have no one to compete against, you could always compete against your best self, and that would work as well. Push yourself to surpass your personal best every day. You can do this by measuring your current results against your results from the past and gauge improvement from there. The goal is to always be a little better each time.

The Self-Discipline Process

Now that you have a deeper understanding of what goes into self-discipline, and the different nuances of having it, you can move on to practicing having stronger self-disciplinary practices.

Step 1: Define What You Want

You can't go anywhere if you do not first have a destination. This destination can be whatever it is you so desire, however, you have to decide first. All of your efforts have to be channeled towards something, and a goal is a great place to start. To decide the goal, you must first ask yourself these questions.

1. What do I want to become and achieve?
2. What sets of habit do I want to have?
3. What existing attitude do I want to alter?
4. What is the major thing should I focus on?

Step 2: Figure Out What Needs to be Done

If you do not change anything, your goal will just remain a desire, not become something that you could achieve. Aspiration without action is nothing, and when you have nothing, you are back at square one. So once you set a goal, you then have to figure out what changes need to be made in order to reach said goal.

Every time you set a goal, you have to make some changes to your lifestyle to achieve it. These changes may be small, or they may be big, but you still have to make them. Sometimes it is not easy to figure out what you need to change in order to reach your goal, so you should ask yourself these questions:

1. In order for me to reach my goals what particular demeanor should I practice?
2. Are there particular routine that I need to follow to reach my ambition?

You should never sacrifice your values to make some changes. You have to keep those in mind so that you can find a way to work around them and make changes to your lifestyle while still keeping your morals intact.

You are going to change. When you have to strive to reach a goal, you are going to grow into a different person, and that is okay as long as you do not let it change you for the worse. You can change for the better. In fact, it is encouraged that you do. Everyone needs to grow sometimes. Even if it means leaving some people behind that are dragging you down. When you go to achieve a goal, ask yourself these questions to determine how much you are going to change:

1. What kind of person should I be for me to reach my goals?
2. What essential traits should I have?
3. In what what way shall I think about myself, my life and my goals?

It is important that you ask yourself these questions, as it gives you a boost towards knowing how the final outcome is going to look when you complete your goal, and you will be able to judge your progress throughout every step of your journey.

Step 3: Find Role Models

Once you have searched inside of yourself for the motivation and commitment to your goal, you must then look outward for someone who can help you stay motivated and merely a source of your inspiration. For example, if you are looking for inspiration to get fit, Dwayne Johnson is a great role model. He hits the gym every day at four AM, no matter his schedule. This is just an example of what to look for when it comes to inspiration. Here are some questions you can reflect to?

1. Are there people practicing it? If so, who are they?
2. Who is it that effectively accomplished this objective?
3. Who is it that effectively aced this routine?
4. Who is it that effectively rolled out this improvement?
5. Who is that practice the essential methods?
6. What would I be able to gain from this individual that can help me towards my progress?

Step 4: Distinguish Reasons and Obstacles

You are going to have obstacles in your life, and you are going to need reasons to get around them. You have to be prepared to fight along the way to get to where you are trying to go. If it was an easy ride to the top, that would not be much of a goal, now would it. Here are some questions you should ask yourself so you can be sort of prepared to reach your goals.

1. What possible obstacles could come my way in achieving my goals?
2. What things could distract me on my journey towards my goal?

If you do not have a lot of compelling reasons to fight an obstacle, you are going to be less likely to keep pushing once you hit a wall. You want to have a reason to keep pushing on, so here are some questions that you should ask yourself about your goal, to remind you of what you are trying to achieve in the first place.

1. Why particularly would I like to accomplish this objective?
2. Why particularly would I like to build up this routine?
3. Why is this significant for me?
4. What will I benefit in accomplishing this?
5. Why do I truly need this?

Answer these questions earnestly, so you can truly see where you need a little more inspiration. Lying to yourself will get you nowhere.

Step 5: Develop Plan of Action

What was the phrase we used earlier? Oh yeah, "Aspiration without action is nothing." Well, here is where you would start to set things into motion and start acting on your goal. However, action without a plan is chaos. You need to take the time to develop a plan of action to help keep you on track. Of course, there will be some obstacles that you can't foresee, but if you have a guideline of where you are supposed to be for every step of the way, it is easier for you to keep on the right track.

When building a plan of action, you should make sure that it is detailed enough that you can hold yourself accountable using it. This can be done by having a set end date to reach your goal and mini milestones along the way. This way you can work on your goal in small bits, and you will know that you are staying on the timeline well. Having an end date for your goal will help you hold yourself accountable if you start falling behind. It will give you the extra push you need to complete your goal.

Step 6: Make Yourself Accountable

As we spoke of earlier, it all comes down to accountability. You have to be able to hold yourself to a high enough standard to complete your goal. If you are not able to do that, you will have to learn how to before you can get anywhere in life.

While a support team is a great thing to have, at the end of the day, you are the one who is responsible for your success and your failure. You have to be responsible enough to take control of your actions.

You have to be your own voice of motivation. No one else can travel the journey for you. If you are able to hold yourself accountable, then you will be able to achieve your goal with ease.

Strengthening Your Self-Discipline

This section may seem a little redundant, but it is necessary to go over more in depth some of the topics that have already been touched on. This will make it easier for you to see the importance of some of these topics that may seem unimportant at this time.

Commit Wholeheartedly

Committing to your goal with all of your heart is a major key to self-discipline. This gives you the biggest reason to keep pushing on if you can hold yourself accountable. If you can't then you will find that it is hard to hold on to your commitment, which can cause some problems.

You can make a personal commitment, or you can make a public commitment. While a public commitment may seem like it is the easiest to keep, that may not be the truth. Often times, those around us may find themselves discouraging us from achieving our goals due to a feeling of inadequacy amongst themselves. It is much easier to keep a personal commitment because you will be able to build yourself up, rather than depending on others to build you up instead.

Committing yourself to your goal does not mean you will automatically succeed though. You have to have a more detailed commitment than "I will get this done."

You have to commit yourself not only to your goal but to do what it takes to achieve your goal. To find the steps that you can take to make achieving your goal that much more possible. If you are not committing yourself fully, then you may not make your goal.

Commit yourself to consistency. You have to be consistent in your daily habit changes to achieve your goal. If you lack consistency, it is so much easier to fall back into your old ways than it is to keep yourself moving towards your goal.

Self-Disciplined State of Mind

There are certain qualities you must take on in order to have a highly self-disciplined state of mind. Optimism, patience, and diligence are the three most important states of mind. You need these to be successful with having a self-disciplined mindset. Optimism, because you have to believe in yourself. Pessimists set themselves up to fail. Patience, because a goal is not reached overnight, and you have to stick with your progress and be patient knowing you will get there. Diligence, because you have to want to stick with yourself and reach your goal.

You have to be committed to consistency as well. If you are not committed to consistency, you will be more likely to slip back into your old ways.

Here are some questions you should ask yourself to help you solidify your mindset:

1. Is there something that I appreciate about this development?
2. Is this energizing?
3. Is this beneficial for me, how?
4. In what way can this undertaking be gratifying?

Visualize Your Desired Outcomes

Visualization is the best thing to help you stay focused on your goal. You have to be able to see yourself moving forward with every step. Visualization is key to reaching your desired goal.

Creating a Supportive Environment

Your environment is almost as important as your mindset. This means that you should surround yourself with a supportive environment. If your environment is toxic and unsupportive, then you will always struggle to stay motivated because those around you will be trying to bring you down. The environment also does not always mean people; it can also mean habits that you have and things that are around your house that may be derailing to your goal.

Observe your surroundings then pose this inquiries:

1. What are the appropriate routines should I practice to accomplish my objective?
2. Is the setting I am in does not distract me from accomplishing my objective?
3. What are the things that I should alter so that I can achieve a steady condition?

The setting you are in must be conducive to making your changes. Otherwise, you will struggle to do so.

Organize Actions

You have to make a list of what has to be done first, and what can be done last. People tend to push off the hard stuff, and do the easy stuff first, which makes them feel accomplished, so they cut out early before doing the hard stuff, and the harder stuff always gets pushed to the side.

Tracking Your Progress

Imagine you were doing great on your goals. You were almost there, and then you suddenly gave up. What would cause you to give up? If you answered "not seeing results" you are in a group of the majority of people who give up on their goal. There is a common picture that is shared around that shows two miners. One is working towards the giant diamond furiously; the other is turning away defeated, just inches away from breaking through to the prize.

This is what happens to a lot of people with a goal. They keep pushing towards their goal, without even looking at how far they have come, and then they give up just shy of reaching their goal because they feel like they are not making any progress at all.

That is why it is important to track the progress you are making and mark down any mini milestones that you hit.

This will keep you focused on your goal, and you will see that you are getting close to your goal. Pushing on without thought can be detrimental to you in the end.

Knowing how to improve your train of thought is one thing, but knowing that it can and has been done is another. Here is an example of a well-known famous person who had a hard time organizing his thoughts.

Albert Einstein

As a young boy, Einstein was written off as illiterate because he was dyslexic. Dyslexia did not only affect how he read, but it also affected how he thought as well. Often times he had a hard time keeping his train of thought on track. He would feel like his entire thought process was derailing as soon as it started. However, he worked hard at keeping himself focused on one thing at a time. He found his strength in science, which made it easier to want to focus.

From there, he disciplined his mind into obeying him. While he still had problems sometimes with getting off track, he was able to think a lot more clearly and come up with some of the best scientific discoveries known to man.

It would be a great idea for you to read up on Einstein. More about him can be found here:
https://en.wikipedia.org/wiki/Albert_Einstein.

Chapter 4: Learning

When you acquire new information, you are learning. Learning is noted as the act of taking in information to understand a new subject. This means that any time you gain an understanding of something you did not previously know, you are learning. Learning is important in the human culture because we are not born with as many instincts as most animals are. Humans have to learn everything from how to communicate to how to walk, and how to function in their society.

Humans learn in a much different way than animals. They learn through education mostly. Someone teaches them what he or she needs to know directly, and often times the learning occurs outside of the home after a certain age. Unlike with animals, where the parents teach the young everything that they need to know to be out on their own.

However, children tend to learn through play which is similar to how animal young learn as well.

Children are known to learn through educational games, sensory play, and kinetic play. This means that they can learn sitting down, touching things, and moving. Pretty much any game a child plays serves some type of learning purpose.

Rote learning

Another main way that humans learn is through rote learning. This is a form of memorization that causes you to commit what you are learning to your long-term memory. Chapter one goes over all of what you need to know about long-term memory, so understanding how that works will give you a better understanding of how rote learning works.

Unfortunately, everyone is different, and there are no set ways to improve your learning skills. You just have to try different things until you find what works for you. It is a system of trial and error, but once you find the right niche, stick with it.

If you feel like you are alone in the learning department, you might be happy to know that the person who is considered to be one of the world's smartest men had issues with learning.

Stephen Hawking

Stephen Hawking suffers from a condition known as ALS, or Amyotrophic Lateral Sclerosis. It has taken over his entire body so that the only thing that works is his mind. He talks through a computer, and all of his movements are controlled through that computer which instructs a chair to move. Despite his difficulties, he is one of the world's most renowned philosophers and is quite the intellectual. He was not always that way.

While he was always deemed smart, he had a fall in his early college years where he struck his head. This was said to trigger his ALS. He began to forget things that he once knew so well, and had to relearn a lot. If he could go from having borderline amnesia to becoming one of the world's smartest men, you too can learn more about the world around you. It would be a great idea to read more about the man, so here is a link where you can find more information: http://www.hawking.org.uk/about-stephen.html

Chapter 5: Attention Span

Your attention span is directly linked to being able to self-discipline your mind, which is discussed in an earlier chapter. Attention span refers to the amount of time you can focus on one thing at a time, and how well you can do while focusing.

A lot of people have a hard time focusing, so they find that they have to work harder to get their work done. However, there are ways to improve your attention span and focus, and here are some tips.

How to Improve your Attention Span and Focus

Many people struggle day in and day out with being able to properly focus on their daily tasks. If you are one of these people, you are not alone, and there are other people in the world who are going through the same problem. In fact, over

80% of the world's population has trouble concentrating from time to time in varying degrees. Some people have problems focusing daily, while others tend to only have problems if they have a lot on their plates. Whatever the reason, you can beat the distractions and regain laser-like focus just by knowing how it works, and have some tips on how to keep yourself on track.

Environment

Most people feel like they have to work with what they are given. This is not conducive to a focused environment. You can make adjustments to your workspace to help you focus so that you can be more productive from the start of each day.

Make sure you're comfortable

Not many people pay much mind to the chairs they sit in at work. However, this can play a big role in your focus. If you are uncomfortable, you may get up to move around more than you need to, which takes time away from your work. A little movement is okay, but the constant movement is a distraction in itself. Make sure your chair is the right height, and get a special cushion if it is too hard.

Put up pictures

You may think that pictures would be distracting. This is where you would be slightly wrong. Pictures with words are distracting, but tranquil landscapes and zen pictures are great for productivity and focus because they do not give you something to focus on, but rather something to help you enjoy your space, so you are more likely to focus.

Shut out distractions as much as possible

Some people use earplugs, while others use music. The key is to use music that doesn't have words. Celtic or Classical music is great for concentration because it drowns out noise from the office allowing you to focus on your work.

Nutrition

What you put in your body has the ability to affect how you focus as well. Nutrition plays a big role in brain function, and if your brain does not have the proper nutrition, it will not want to function the way it should.

Drink water

It is super important to drink water. You have to drink water to stay hydrated. If you are dehydrated, it could lead to a lack of concentration which would take down your productivity. The brain needs water to function. Without it, you could feel tired, sluggish, or ill. None of these are conducive to a high concentration environment.

Don't Skip Your Meals

You have to make sure that you are feeding your brain so that it can properly focus. If you are hungry, your stomach will send signals to your brain, interfering with the information you are trying to take in. This leads to multiple distractions, whereas you would be distraction free on a satisfied stomach.

Get up and move around

While moving too much is a distraction, not moving enough can be one too. Your body gets anxious when it is idle for too long because it puts stress on your joints. Getting up once an hour and stretching for about five minutes is a great way to maintain focus on the task at hand.

Mindset

Mind over matter is another way to handle focus difficulties. Even if you have a problem with concentrating due to a disorder, you can still improve your focus by taking control of your mind. This will allow you to focus more than you ever thought was possible.

Set aside time to deal with worries

Worrying is the number one productivity killer. Many people have worries outside the office, and these can eat up your thoughts for most of the day, making it difficult to focus. You have to leave your home life and stress at the door in order to focus on the tasks at hand. Later on in this book will be information on balancing your work and home life for better focus.

Focus on one task at a time

Multitasking is viewed as the number one way to be productive, but science has proved this is the opposite of the truth when it comes to focusing and quality. You have to take the time to do one task at a time in order to truly be able to focus on what you are doing. When you try to spread your focus out, it gets harder to keep track of what you are doing, and it can cause quality to suffer.

Close your email box and chat program

Your email can wait for an allotted time slot for replies. Your clients, boss, cousin's aunt, whoever can wait until you have time to answer your email. Same goes for your phone. Put it on silent, and only answer it when the time comes around.

This will allow you to work with minimal interruptions so you can focus on what you are doing.

Switch between high- and low-attention tasks

Many people try to prioritize their work from high to low. They work on the high importance projects first and leave the low importance projects for last. This can cause you to bog down after a few tasks because your brain does not have time to rest until all of the high importance tasks are finished. By alternating high and low tasks, your brain gets a break, and you can focus for longer. This allows you to get more tasks accomplished in less time.

Prioritize

Not having a list of things to do is killer on your focus, because you have to spend time on each task figuring out what to do next, and it takes a toll on your brain having to double check each time to make sure that you do not forget anything. By spending a few minutes at the beginning of each workday to make a list of what needs to be done, and prioritizing it in an offset manner as mentioned above, you will find that you increase your productivity tenfold.

More Tips for Improving Your Concentration

Take short breaks

Focusing intensely for eight hours feels impossible, and to be honest, it nearly is. Break up your focus sessions into one-hour blocks, and allow yourself five to ten minutes in between to give your brain a break. This will help you be able to maintain a constant level of focus for all of your tasks, and you won't feel your mind start to wander as bad towards the end of the day.

Do your hardest tasks when you're most alert

During different times of the day, you will be more alert. These times generally fall just before, and just after lunch. This should be the time when you do your hardest tasks because it will be easier for you to focus then. If you try to do them first thing, when your brain is still getting into gear, it will be a lot harder to maintain the level of focus that the task needs.

Use a phone headset

No, you don't actually make calls, you just put the headset on, and continue your work to fool your coworkers into thinking you are busy. This will keep them from trying to interrupt you so that you can work distraction free. A "do not disturb" sign works well too.

Promise yourself a reward

Giving yourself a reward is a great way to stay motivated to focus. It can be simple such as work for an hour and get a snack from the vending machine if you are successful. The trick is to hold yourself accountable if you do not meet your goal. No goal, no reward.

Schedule email downloads

Let's face it. Emails come in at the most inconvenient times. This can become a distraction as you may be tempted to check them constantly. As noted above, you should set aside a time of day to answer emails. Once you decide on a time, schedule your email downloads for that time.

Think of Your Mind as a Muscle

Your mind is more than an organ. It is a muscle as well. It can pull heavy workloads just like your arms and back can, only these ones are mental rather than physical. You should think of your mind as one of your most important muscles in order to care for it properly.

Just like your physical muscles, your brain requires exercise. You have to work out your brain for it to stay strong and sharp. This happens during the work day when you have to focus. However, if you overexert your brain, it can make it harder for it to do its job. Just like if you try to bench press too much weight, you can injure your arms. You need to know the limits of your brain and slowly work on increasing those limits, but your brain needs rest too.

Have you ever felt a feeling of dread before starting the work day? Do you feel the same feeling before an intense workout? This just goes to show that your brain is a muscle in itself. You may go in feeling like you can't do it, but with the proper form and function, you will be able to do the entire process with ease.

You can hit a wall with your concentration same as you can with a workout. When you hit this wall, you just have to dig a little deeper to find the motivation to push through. Maybe the promise of a reward will help. Nonetheless, you have to work hard to strengthen your brain. Here are some tips that will help you do just that so that the tips above seem more feasible.

11 Exercises That Will Strengthen Your Attention

The first thing you should know is that just reading this section is not going to help you at all. You can read all you want, but if you do not put these things into action, you will find that it is not going to do a thing for your focus. You will still be at the same level of attention you always were. So read, but also act upon what you have read.

1. Increase the strength of your focus gradually:

Focus is not gained overnight. You have to work hard to achieve it. Most people will throw themselves into a fury trying to gain it all in one day. It doesn't work like that. Just as you have to build up your stamina to get into shape, you have to build up your mental stamina as well. If you go from having trouble focusing for twenty minutes to trying to focus for eight hours, you are not going to get anywhere. You have to pace yourself.

Start out with a simple goal. Set a timer for an hour. If you work completely focused for one hour, you can treat yourself to a five-minute break. However, every time you find your mind wandering during the hour you should be focusing, you have to restart until you can make it an hour without surfing the web.

2. Create a distraction to-do list:

Distractions can be a pain. Your own mind will be working against you. With technology today being so advanced, we can get answers to any question that pops into our heads instantly. This makes it hard to not just pop over to a separate tab and look up what we want to know, but this takes you off task.

Try writing down the questions that you have if they are not work related. Once you hit your break time, you can then answer those questions and ease your mind. This prevents you from spending twenty-five minutes trying to get back on task when you break your concentration.

3. Build your willpower:

Later on in this book, we will talk about how to build your self-discipline. This can help your focus because the two are entwined. You have to have the willpower to keep yourself on track, and you have to have the focus to maintain willpower.

4. Meditate.

Meditation is a great way to improve mindfulness. It will help you clear your mind of any type of worry or possible distraction that could pop up. Before you start your workday, spend fifteen minutes meditating to clear your mind so that you can focus on the day ahead, rather than what you were worried about last night.

Studies have shown that meditation creates a vast improvement in focus. If you can focus on thinking of nothing for fifteen minutes, it will be a lot easier to focus on one thing for an hour or more. You will be able to block out intruding thoughts to maintain the focus you need to get through the day.

5. Practice mindfulness throughout the day:

In addition to meditation at the beginning of each day, you should spend your entire day dedicating yourself to a more mindful existence. This will help you focus not only on work but at home as well. Again, later on in the book, you will learn the importance of a work and home balance and how to separate the two completely.

You can practice mindfulness when you are eating. Focus on each bite. Count the number of times that you chew before you swallow. Note the flavors of the food you are consuming, and really enjoy what you are eating. This will allow you to raise your focus in all that you do.

This can also help you protect yourself from invading thoughts. When you have the urge to do something else, you can just think to yourself that you need to stay on task, and it will become easier to do so.

6. Exercise

You may wonder what exercising your body has to do with focus, but the truth is they can tie in together very nicely. Just as you have to push through a concentration barrier when working, you have to push through a rigorous workout. This will help you strengthen your willpower, which you can use when you are trying to focus. It is a great way to help your body and your mind.

7. Memorize stuff

Make it a point to memorize one thing each week. Whether it be a poem or a quote. Memorizing things will help you work on focusing on something over a long period of time. It takes a lot of focus to commit something to memory, so the more you can commit to memory, the less you have to worry about when it comes to focusing on something that is right in front of you.

8. Read long stuff slowly.

Part of focusing means to read everything thoroughly. Most people nowadays look for the summary of everything. There are even websites to give you the synopsis of a book so that you don't have to read the whole book yourself. This really makes your focusing skills take a hit because you are not forced to focus for long periods of time to get an answer to a question.

This need for instant gratification is becoming a culture, and focus and attention spans are suffering horribly for it. By reading a long article, or a long book, you will be strengthening your focus, because you stuck with it. The more you read, the better your attention span will be, because the two things are directly linked together.

9. Stay Curious

Keep yourself on the up and up by being intrigued by things. Many people feel like curiosity is a trait for children, and adults should just know things. However, you don't know everything. By striving to try, you will have more of a reason to stay focused on tasks at hand, and you will be more likely to have a higher attention span.

They say curiosity killed the cat, but the lack of curiosity killed intellect. You have to maintain a level of curiosity to be interested enough to pursue anything. If you do not have any interest, it is going to be harder to focus, because everything will seem unimportant to you. You have to look at every task as an opportunity to learn. This will help you maintain a level of focus that not a lot of people have these days.

10. Practice attentive listening.

The number one complaint people have about conversing with others is a person's inability to truly listen. We are a society where we listen to respond, rather than to comprehend. This takes minimal focus to do. You have to listen with all of your focus when talking with someone. Otherwise, you will not be listening at all. When you practice attentive listening, not only will it be easier to focus as time goes on, you will find that you can connect with people a lot easier than you used to.

11. Perform concentration exercises

Again, just reading these things does not do you any good. You have to actively practice them. By performing these exercises and more, you will find that you can improve your attention span significantly. You can impress your boss, your

Chapter 5: Attention Span

lover, and your friends by being more productive, and more attentive.

The modern world has become the enemy to true attention. All of the technology we have today makes it so easy to do things halfway without using our brains. That is why robots are so popular. People love the idea of not having to do anything for themselves. However, their focus and attention suffer. They find that when they do need to focus on a task, it is nearly impossible. This is due to all of the distractions that technology presents. Now it is more important than ever to make sure that you are working to maintain and improve your focus so that you never have to suffer again from a lack of attention span.

Of course, there are other ways to improve your attention span as well. Some people are just looking for a way to focus long enough to get their work done. Other people are wanting to know how to delve deeply into their work in order to truly enjoy focusing on their tasks. Below are some tips on how to focus almost as if you were a monk on your daily work.

There is a moment in time that everyone strives to have at some point in his or her life. They strive to get so lost in their work that the world around them disappears. Sometimes this stems from a need to escape their everyday life, and sometimes it is just a need for more focus to get a high volume of work done. Whatever the reason, you have probably wished this more than once, with no idea how to achieve it. This is known as finding your work zen. It refers to the monk-like focus that people can get into when they are working on a project. It is attainable for everyone. If you wish to find your state of zen, then you need only to read and live these steps below. It takes some practice, but it is worth it to have a more peaceful work life.

Everyone struggles from time to time when it comes to maintaining focus. That is nothing to be ashamed of. However, if it regularly impedes with your work, then you should strive to become better at focusing. This entire chapter is filled with tips on how to do so, and here are even more. These tips are for people who struggle with attention deficiency. By immersing themselves in their work, they can

Chapter 5: Attention Span

really get a lot done without distractions. Even if you do not struggle with this, you too can benefit from a zen-like focus.

Psychologist Susan Perry has a lot of information on how focus works, and it is her expertise that this section is using to help create tips to find your zen. While you could talk to real monks, it is best to know not only how to achieve something, but the science behind it as well to quell the skeptics. However, next time, we may ask a real monk just to see how similar the answers are.

There are two things you should know about before we get into how to make your focus so steeply that you find yourself enjoying getting lost in your work. You should know what happens when you focus, and also what happens when you break your focus. Knowing both of these will help you later on when you go to apply what you know to your own work.

Why Focusing is Significant?

It all starts with a question. "What do you want to focus on?" This is the question the brain sends you in the form of a signal. Once you have decided the task you wish to focus on; your brain starts the process of sorting and identifying the object at hand. This allows your brain to discern what needs to be focused on from outside information that would merely distract you.

Mentally you create a picture of what you need to focus on, and visually you take in all of the information in front of you. Your brain is like a camera for information. It blurs the background, leaving the subject in focus. This helps you focus longer and harder on the subject at hand.

From there, you focus more on what you need to in order to get the job done. It is almost like a zoom lens. You zoom in on one portion of the project at a time, eliminating distracting details until it is their turn to have your focus.

Once you have established strong enough focus, you will be in the zone. This will make it easier for you to forget the world around you other than what you are working on. Many people can stay this way for hours until something manages to sneak in and distract them.

Studies show that both the left and right brain seem to work together when it comes to focusing. However, it is hard to get a proper MRI of the brain when it is functioning as people tend to be moving around during that time.

What Happens if You Get Distracted?

While top-down attention, which controls your focus, can be controlled and manipulated, the same can't be said for bottom-up attention. This is what you use to break concentration and allow distractions in. It is hard-wired into our brains to allow distractions as a safety measure. If humans were to get too distracted, they could be placed in dangerous situations without realizing it. Such as not noticing the house is on fire or some other danger like that. So there are some things that cannot be ignored when you are focusing.

Two things are able to break your focus. Bright lights, and loud sounds. These two things are tied to dangerous situations, such as gunshots and police lights and sirens.

Primitively it was animal growls and lighting strikes or fire. Our brains are hardwired to notice these things even when we are locked onto something else.

Once you break focus, it takes around twenty-five minutes to regain it back. This is because you have to restart the whole process of getting back into the in-depth focus. If you find yourself exhausted at the end of the day, you actually are becoming exhausted by the distractions around you because your brain is getting tired of having to reset itself to focus.

Attention spans are like water glasses. When they are calm, it is easy to see straight through them. However, when they are disturbed, it takes a while for things to calm back down enough to see clearly again.

No two people are the same, and some people can work with things in the background that would be disastrously distracting for their coworker. Some people can work with loud music in the background, and other people have to have complete silence to even get a minimal amount of work done. Everyone is different, but there are some distractions that everyone suffers from.

Identify What Triggers Distraction and Eliminate Them

There are two things that we are evolutionarily designed to be distracted by. These two things are loud sounds and blinking lights. Pretty much everyone is distracted by these two things to some degree, due to it being part of a mechanism in our brains that is meant to keep us safe.

There are a lot of ways to block out the potential for distractions. You just have to find what works for you. Here are some ideas of things that can help.

Noise canceling headphones or earplugs are a great way to cancel out any distracting noises that may come your way. It is important that you remember that noises may not always be directed at you but they can still be distracting if they are loud enough. Someone shouting across the room to their friend, a car going down the street with loud music blasting, all of these things have the potential to distract you. Make sure you are aware of the noisiest times of the day so that you can be prepared and know when to use your noise blocking devices.

Timed internet blocks can be a definite help to you. We have already noted to have your email downloads scheduled, but you can also block certain web pages during certain times of the day as well. This will prevent notifications from popping up, and even if you are tempted to check your social media sites or email, you will not be able to because you are blocked from doing so. This is a great tool for those who are still working on the willpower thing.

Control Your Mind to Get Rid of Internal Distractions

Everyone has some internal distractions every now and then. The distraction can be a variety of things. Such as why someone is not answering your calls, or what you are going to eat for dinner. Maybe even some weekend plans you are looking forward to. All of these things have the ability to derail you from your work in a whirlwind of daydreams and annoying little ear worms that keep playing through your head.

The best thing to do is to set up your environment to eliminate outside distractions. This will give you a place to feel like you are separate from what is going on in the outside world, so you can truly focus on the tasks at hand.

You have to identify the distractions before they begin to take hold. If you know you are buzzing about the weekend ahead, schedule a time to think of it. This will tell your brain "I know you are excited, and we will get to it, but this is more important right now" so that you can focus. Little things like that involve you taking control of your own mind so that you can truly find peace in your work with minimal distraction.

Find a Scientific Way to Maximize Your Focus

There are many different scientifically-backed ways to maximize your focus. The simplest way? Play brain games. There are several out there for many different consoles and platforms. These games will help you expand your mind, and there are ones designed specifically for focusing. They will help you focus more on your work and help you feel like you have a clearer mind when it comes to concentrating.

Get Entertained

How many times have you been told to relax to benefit your work life? Never? Well, today is your lucky day. Find something that is entertaining to do. Here is the kicker. It has to be something that is not too easy.

There is a difference between being lost in something, and being productive. When you are just lost in something, you could be elsewhere entirely mentally, which could cause some quality flaws in your work. When you are productive, you are lost in your work, but mentally with what you are doing. The only difference is once the world melts away you stay with your present task. It can be hard to get lost in something and stay focused on the task at hand, but it is possible with practice. You do this with forms of entertainment.

While any type of entertainment can do, some are better than others. Television only works if you have advertising free television. This way the ads will not break your concentration on the program at hand. It works best with an online television service because you can follow the plot of movies without interruptions, and shows as well. However, it is advised that you stay away from television if possible because it can be hard to truly focus on television as your mind tends to wander. It is best to go with a good book, or a video game, or a board game such as chess. These require attentive focus, and it is easier to tell when your mind is trying to wander.

Remember, these tips will not make you perfect at focusing on their own. You have to practice actively on them all the time.

Chapter 6: Another Relatable Inspiration - Thomas Edison

An inventor, genius, businessman, and a household name. These are probably all things you think about when you think Thomas Edison. However, there was much more to him than that. He was a family man as well. You will learn later on in this book about his marriages and his children.

He was a very driven man and a very hard worker. Sometimes too hard of a worker. He would get excited about something, and tended to dive right in. He often times did not stop to think about the best way to do things and expended a lot more effort than necessary, but he still got the job done.

He was very passionate about the things that he did. He would not accept anything less than perfect. Often times he would revise an idea so many times that it was unrecognizable from the beginning plan. This was the kind of man he was. He tried over and over to achieve perfection in everything that he did.

When you think of Edison, you probably think of the light bulb, but the man was so much more than just one invention. He was the father of recordable and playable music. He invented so many useful things that we still use a form of today. He was the instrument in technology.

He held many patents throughout the world and was very well known in many countries. A very affluent man, he was well-respected by many. However, he did have a major flaw. He was very stingy and did not like to spend much more than he absolutely had to. He often underpaid his staff and overworked them.

While he was not a perfect person, there is no disputing that the man was a powerful inventor, and without him, we would not have a lot of the stuff that we had today. So without further ado, let us continue on with learning more about the man who brought us light in the darkest hours, Mr. Thomas Edison.

Who Was He

On February eleventh, 1847, an infant came into the world in the town of Milan, Ohio. Little did the parents know that they had given birth to a legend. Born under the name Thomas Alva Edison, he was the youngest of seven children, and quite possibly, the brightest.

Edison was homeschooled by his mother, and much of his learning came from reading. Edison was an avid reader, often reading the most boring of manuscripts to gain more knowledge. Stuff that would put you or me to sleep was what kept him up at night. There was no amount of information that was not worth learning.

Early in his childhood, Edison was struck by a variety of ailments. He got hit with scarlet fever, which he survived, and he had several inner ear infections that were often left untreated. This caused him to have a substantial hearing loss that he would later in life make up wild stories to explain.

Edison's family was not rich; they were actually pretty poor. So poor that when the railroad started to bypass Milan, they had to move for work. They moved all the way to Port Huron, Michigan, and that was when Edison had to start working to help supplement the family income. He worked two jobs, selling newspapers and candies on the railroad from Port Huron to Detroit, and he also sold vegetables as well. As he worked on the railroad, he started doing experiments in empty boxcars. Unfortunately, one of his experiments went awry, and he caught a boxcar on fire. This was when he began the rumors about his hearing loss. He attributed it to the conductor pulling him out of the train by his ears, and boxing them as he got off at the station.

After the railroad, Edison decided to go solo on his newspaper expeditions. The newspaper company he worked for agreed, as they did not want any more mishaps like the one on the train to be their responsibility. He gathered up a few friends, and together they printed their own paper to sell the papers that they were already selling. The paper they sold, the Grand Trunk Herald, did so well that Edison began to see a future as an entrepreneur. In fact, eventually, he became such a good businessman that he started up fourteen successful businesses. One of which is still a major brand today, and you may have a product in your home right now. The General Electric brand, or GE for short.

On one of his paper expeditions, Edison saved a three-year-old boy from being hit by a train that had derailed and was careening out of control in their direction. The father of the boy was so pleased and grateful that he offered Edison a job on the spot. Edison agreed and was trained to be a telegraph operator at once. He worked for a while in Port Huron, but once he was ready to go it alone, he took a telegraphing job in Ontario.

When Edison turned nineteen, he took off for Louisville. Yes, Louisville Kentucky. The farthest away from Ontario he could have possibly gone it seems. He took a job with the Western Union. One of the country's largest telegraphing companies around. He worked the night shift of the news wire, and since in those days not much went on at night, he had plenty of time for reading. With reading, came experimenting, and when an experiment went wrong, he got fired. Oh, poor Edison, he never learned not to mix business and science.

After he had been fired in Kentucky, he moved to Elizabeth, New Jersey. Here he found a mentor that allowed Edison to live in the basement of his home until he established himself. Franklin Leonard Pope was a telegrapher and inventor like Edison, but with more knowledge. Once Edison had begun learning from Pope, he started working on his own inventions. At this point in time, his inventions mainly dealt with telegraphy, such as a stock ticker. However, his first patent was for an electric vote counter. His patent was granted shortly after he turned twenty-one.

Shortly after he got his first patent, he opened up a few shops. They were pretty successful, and he was even able to hire a few employees. One of which was Mary Stillwell. Edison fell for her the moment he met her in his shop, and two months later, they were married. They had been

Chapter 6: Another Relatable Inspiration - Thomas Edison

married for two years when their first child arrived. Marion Estelle Edison was their first born child, and she was nicknamed Dot. Three years later, they had a boy. They named him Thomas Alva Edison Jr and gave him the nickname Dash. (Seeing the telegraph theme here?) Two years after the birth of little Dash, they had another son by the name of William Leslie Edison. He had no nickname but is the only one which is documented to have gone to college. He also followed in his father's footsteps and became an inventor.

Sadly, at age 29 and after thirteen short years of marriage, Mary died of unknown causes. Some attribute it to a possible brain tumor, but it was more likely that she died of morphine poisoning, as it was a common medicine in those days, and no one knew the ghastly side effects yet. So that left Edison to raise three pre-adolescent children on his own. However, he continued to invent and still was a great father to his children.

He would not have to raise them alone, however, as just two short years later, he married Mina Miller, the daughter of

Lewis Miller, an inventor that Edison both admired and respected. They had three children together as well. A girl and two boys just like the with his previous wife. The children were, Madeleine Edison, and she grew up to marry John Eyre Sloane. Charles Edison, governor of New Jersey from 1941-1944, and who later took on his father's businesses when he passed, and Theodore Miller Edison, who graduated out of MIT's Physics Department, and has more than eighty patents accredited to him. This time, Edison's wife outlived him, and they were married at the end of his days.

In his early days, Edison had several inventions that went unnoticed. He had many devices for improving telegraphic function, such as his automatic repeater, but no one really attributed those to his name. However, in 1877, he invented the phonograph. It was the biggest invention that he had ever created, and had more success than he had ever dreamed possible at this point in time. Most people thought that it had to be magical, and called Edison the Wizard of Menlo Park. It recorded sound on tinfoil around circular grooves and was only used for a few plays. Nonetheless, the public was smitten with this device, and it got Edison recognized across the nation. He even got invited to the White House to showcase his invention. However, he did not expand on the phonograph. Further, it was not until Alexander Graham Bell took over the idea that it was made to be any better than it was when Edison first designed it.

Edison designed a quadruplex telegraph and sold it to the Western Union. He was surprised that they offered him ten thousand dollars for the invention, and graciously accepted. It gave him the funds he needed to build an industrial research lab in Menlo Park. It was his first shop that was designed to bring out constant innovation in technology. While Edison had people to do a lot of the research and development, they did only under his instruction.

Edison was known for being hard on his workers, paying them low wages and making them work extra-long hours until they had a task finished. However, his workers learned much, and some were able to even go and get their own patents. If a worker did a good job, they were praised, and often got a raise depending on the amount of work they did.

However, the raises were often minor. Thus, Edison was portrayed as a cruel boss and a stingy man.

Edison hired William Joseph Hammer in 1879. Hammer was instrumental in Edison's design of electric incandescent lamps. Hammer was promoted to chief engineer of Edison Lamps Works. In his first year, he produced fifty thousand lamps, and impressed Edison, earning the title, Pioneer of Incandescent Electric Lighting. Under Hammer's prompting, Edison hired Frank J. Sprague, a valued mathematician who handled the mathematical aspects of the research, as Edison was not prone to using mathematics himself. However, when his other workers brought up great mathematical values, he was known to use them in his designs to help make them better, as he was not averse to math, he just preferred not to do it himself.

Edison was known to have employed some of the greatest minds of history. It is no surprise with the fact that eventually his research lab expanded over two city blocks, and had almost every material conceivable to the human mind, and some only known to squirrels (the latter may or may not be true.) His lab was not the only one to be in existence though, as more were going to be built later on in his life.

During Edison's early years, while many boys were out working to help bring home food for their family, Edison was becoming an inventor on top of doing multiple jobs to keep bringing in income. There are many different accounts of him losing his jobs due to experimenting while working, but he always found another job shortly after that.

It was in these years that Edison started his own businesses, and found he was a great businessman and was very savvy. That is a feat for most young men. They are just beginning to learn what trade they are good in, and still have years to go before they open their own shops, but Edison had already opened a few. That is due in part to him not having to do a long apprenticeship, as electricity was still a fairly new concept, and people who knew how to work with it were few and far between. This left a good open market for those who wished to get patents and start a business up in the field, without having to have a signature of a master.

His Inventions

There are many things that the man invented. And we still use a lot of them today. Some of the inventions, you may not realize that he has created, but they were in fact, his inventions. Here are the inventions of Edison.

Phonograph: This is the oldest version of the record player. It had a large horn on the end that was used as a speaker, and it had to be cranked up to play. The disks it used were circular pieces of tin foil that had sound lines etched into it. A needle dug along the grooves and made the sound come out of the giant horn like the speaker in music form. (If you watch Harry Potter, the fourth movie, Harry Potter and the Goblet of Fire, has a phonograph featured in it when McGonagall is giving lessons on the Yule Ball.) Many people felt that this invention was magical because there had never been anything like it seen before. It was the greatest invention of the time. However, Alexander Graham Bell often gets credit for the phonograph because Edison did not try to better the invention so when the protection limit hit on the patent, Graham Bell took it over and made it better.

When was the last time you listened to music? Today? Yesterday? Chances are, you don't go very long without listening to music. Imagine if the technology wasn't there to listen to the bands that you love, and you would have to go without the songs they sing for long periods of time until you could see them play in person. Well even then, it would be different. They would be using all acoustic equipment, and not many people could attend because there would be no voice amplification. The phonograph was a big stride in recording and playing sound, and if Edison had not come up with the idea, then we would probably not have the musical devices that we have today, and that is a frightening thought.

Electrical Lighting: This is the category that Edison is seemingly most known for. While he was not the first person to try to created incandescent lighting, he was the first to come up with the design of the light bulb as we know it today. He tried many different ideas but was having a lot of trouble making the bulb's light be long lasting. He knew that he had to get high resistance so that the bulb would not need a lot of electricity to put out a light, and when he got that, he had a hard time finding a filament that could hold up to that amount of resistance. However, inspiration hit when he and a few members of his team took a vacation to Wyoming to visit Battle Lakes and watch the total solar eclipse that year. Edison started examining the bamboo on his fishing rod, and that gave him the idea to use a bamboo filament, which would burn for up to twelve hundred hours. Edison hoped that he could rival the lighting of gas and kerosene lamps. Little did he know that he would completely wipe out the need for them in just a few short years.

Edison did a demonstration on his light bulb, and railroad owner that attended wanted Edison to install his lights on the new steamer they were building. Edison agreed, and the Columbia was installed with the first commercial use of the electric lamp created by Edison Electric Light Company.

However, it was not all roses with Edison, as he had many people try to sue him, saying that he used their design, and he had many competitors trying to create what he did for a lot cheaper. Such as induction lighting, which his rival, George Westinghouse bought the patent for. It was cheaper than incandescent lighting, but much more dangerous, and was known to cause fires. However, people were taking the risk to save money. This forced Edison to lower his prices and make his product more affordable on the market.

Think back to a time when you didn't have electric lighting in your house. Chances are, you probably can't remember unless you lived during the dust bowl, and electricity was wiped out in many areas for long times. Electric lamps and light bulbs have become a necessity in our generation. Electricity, in general, is a necessity anymore. If we don't have it, we panic. Our food spoils. We can't get a hold of anyone after a few hours because our phones die. Electricity has become such an important part of our everyday lives, and it is all because Edison made that first stride and did not give up on the idea of incandescent lighting.

Electric Power Distribution: Edison wanted to make electricity as easy to obtain as gas, and so he created a company that distributed electric power much like the gas utilities were distributed. He used the first steam powered electricity distributor, and it used DC current. While electricity was still not widespread house to house, it was a lot easier for the general public to obtain electricity.

However, he had a lot of rivalries with Tesla designing AC power. The alternating currents allowed electricity to travel over hundreds of miles, and reach people even in the rural areas. Tesla sold his patent to Westinghouse, and AC won the game. However, the alternating currents are often too dangerous for certain appliances, so the DC adapter must be used. Such as the brick on your laptop cord.

Fluoroscopy: Edison designed the first ever commercial use fluoroscope. This used x-rays to make an image on a radiograph plate. These calcium tungstate plates were a lot better than the platinocyanide plates that had previously been used as the fluoroscope plates made a way better picture. In fact, they are still used today. However, working around radiation for so long almost cost Edison his eyesight, and killed his assistant who volunteered to be a test subject for Edison. By 1903, he was so afraid of x-ray machines that he even refused to talk about them.

Have you ever broken a bone? Or thought that you had broken one? If you have at some point in your life, you most likely had an Xray done of the afflicted area. The plate that they attach the magnet on is a fluoroscope plate. It is the same type of plate that Edison used to show the x-rays back in the old days, however, now it can be transmitted to the computer, rather than have to stay on the plate. This saves a lot of money because calcium tungstate can get rather expensive. The concept remains the same, however, and thus Edison's work is still used today even in the hospitals.

Telegraph Improvements: Edison grew in the telegraphy business, and it makes sense that some of his first patents were in telegraphy. He made the stock ticker, which was the first telegraph broadcaster that was completely electric based. He also made the first two-way telegraph and a quadruplex telegraph. These allowed him to get into the world of inventing, and even make some money to start his other inventions. The quadruplex telegraph made him the money he needed to build his lab in Menlo Park.

The telegraph was the first way of communication across long distances, and it was very important. Especially during war time. The telegraphs were sent in morse codes, and you had to add a stop after every word. However, during the wartime, sometimes telegraphs would be sent without any stops to confuse the enemy if it fell into the wrong hands. Or the stops would be put in random places. The telegraph was basically an extremely old and very limited email.

Motion Picture Camera: Edison created the very first motion picture camera and the very first motion picture, viewer. The camera or kinetograph was created by WKL Dickson and Edison together. Edison worked on the energy and mechanics of the camera, and Dickinson, a photographer, worked on the optics of the camera.

The kinetoscope was used to view the short films made by the kinetograph.

A bigger version of the kinetoscope, the Vitascope, was used to project these films onto larger screens. An old style projector, if you will. The Vitascope was very popular in New York City, and Edison designed cylinders that you could add voice overs for the films on, and manually synchronize it with the movie.

However, despite the Vitascope being good for a bigger audience, the kinetoscope was the most popular of the two, as it was more suitable for a private setting. It was sold all over the world and made a fortune. Edison made many short films of many different types. In fact, the first Frankenstein was filmed with a kinetograph and shown on the kinetoscopes.

Today, we have high definition televisions and can take videos with our cell phones. Movies come equipped with soundtracks and speaking already recorded on them. These advances would not have even been possible had Edison not thought of making the kinetograph, and just left the thought in the back of his mind. And even if someone did think of the idea, I can imagine things would be very different than they are today.

Those are only some of the inventions that Edison created, but they are some of the most important to our history. He had several minor inventions as well. The man had well over a thousand patents in his name, and very few were ever disputed as being someone else's work.

Edison was also a very savvy businessman. He owned and operated many businesses, and had a hand in a lot more than he owned. There are also some countries that used his name to exploit his genius, and those will be noted in here as well. Here are the companies that Edison was involved in or owned.

Lansden Company: This was an automobile company that Edison owned a good portion of in controlling interest. Eventually, he tired of the automobile industry and sold his interest, and moved on to other companies.

Battery Supplies Company: Former Edison employees started up this company to sell batteries and their accessories. However, they had stolen the ideas from Edison, and he sued them for patent infringement. After a long litigation process, a settlement was reached, and Edison purchased the company, making it his own, and then legally dissolving it three years later.

Deutsche Edison Accumulatoren Company: This was an exploitation company in Berlin. It was backed by the bank, and really had nothing to do with Edison, other than covertly using his name to sell storage batteries.

Edison Gesellschaft: A legal German branch of an Edison company. It sold a lot of his inventions such as the phonograph and kinetoscope. It was managed by Thomas Graf for years. It even ran for a while during the war and kept a small office even after the big company itself absolved. The office continued running until the retirement of Graf.

Edison Manufacturing Company: Edison's personal company. Originally started up to sell primary batteries; it began selling Edison's other inventions as well pretty soon after the beginning. It started in New Jersey and expanded across the country. Eventually, it went to Thomas A Edison Inc. and was dissolved shortly thereafter.

Other Battery Companies: We could go on all day about the many battery companies that Edison was a part of. He would start a company only to dissolve it a few years later when he thought of a better idea. He was not very fond of just fixing what he had; he had to start brand new every time. He had many other minor battery companies that often didn't last more than a year before they were dissolved, and a new one was being created.

Cement Companies: Edison was very big in the Cement company business. He had about five cement company businesses, and they distributed everything from cement itself to architecture and tools to handle the cement. The biggest one of these was the Edison Portland Cement Company. It produced cement all across the US and Canada. It had mills in many places, and while it started in 1899, it did not dissolve until 1931. One of the longest lasting cement companies he ever started.

Okay, we could go all day talking about the companies he owned for a few years, or he had a hand in, but that would take up more time than you probably want to spend reading about the man, no matter how enthralling he may be. The first few were to show you how many times he dissolved a company only to build another one similar immediately thereafter. So from here on out, the most known and biggest companies will be mentioned here.

Edison General Electric: Edison created a general electric company to get electricity to the people. Eventually, he merged with Thomson-Houston and dropped his name from the title, and it was called General Electric company. General Electric is still in use today, providing everything from light bulbs to household appliances. Today it has been shortened to GE for General Electric.

Commonwealth Edison: A fuel company that Edison invested in, and is now known as Exelon.

DTE Energy: Formerly known as Detroit Edison

As you can see, Edison had quite the range of companies. Cement, mining, electric, batteries, telegraphy, and much more. He was a very important investor in many small companies, as well as starting up his own. He started the film industry, and he started the cement business. While he did not succeed in mining, he used his ideas in the field elsewhere in life.

Why this is outstanding

Read this anecdote:

A young boy by the name of Thomas Edison came home from school one day, and in his hand, he carried a note from his teacher. He skipped through the front door, not knowing what was in the note in his hand, for he could not yet read.

"Mamma. I got a note from school today!" He shouted as he ran through the door.

"Oh really, son? Let me see it." She replied, wondering what possibly the teacher could need to write home about.

However, she soon understood, as she read the note in her head. The note read:

Dear Mrs. Edison
I am writing to inform you that your son, Thomas, is addled, and we would no longer like for him to return to school. We cannot handle him.

Sincerely,
His Teacher

Thomas Edison's mother burst into tears, as she could not believe what she was reading. She felt that her son was very bright, and was not, in fact, mentally ill.

"What's wrong Mamma, did I do something bad?" Thomas asked, upon seeing his mother's tears.

"No son. These are tears of joy." She lied quickly. She never wanted her son to know the truth. So she read the note aloud but changed the reason for why he was not to return to school.

"Dear Mrs. Edison: Your son, Thomas is a genius, and we cannot teach him anymore. Please teach him yourself. Sincerely, His teacher."

"Really, Mama? I am a genius?" Thomas asked, astounded.

"Yes, son, you are."

From that moment on, his mother taught him at home. She taught him how to read, despite his dyslexia, and she taught him how to do the math, and how to do science. She taught him a love for the arts and gave him a thirst for knowledge. Eventually, Thomas grew to be a genius, as his mother had once believed he could be. He became enamored with learning and wanted to know everything that he could. Though his family was not rich, he managed to get plenty of reading materials by finding what people had thrown out, such as periodicals and newspapers. He talked to other people a lot and learned from them as well. He was never satisfied with what he knew, rather, he wanted to learn more.

When Thomas was thirteen, his mother passed away. As he was going through her things, he found the letter that his teacher had written, back when he was a little boy. He read the truth for the first time – that he was believed to be mentally ill and was not welcomed back at school. He wrote in his diary later that night.

Thomas Edison was an addled boy, who thanks to a hero mother, became a genius.

Edison never forgot the amount of love his mother gave him that day, by deciding not to listen to the words of a teacher, but rather her own heart, and put in the time and effort to unlock the genius hidden inside of him.

Edison was not the best in school when he was a little boy. He had a hard time reading and a hard time focusing. He could not stay on one task at a time, and for this, his teachers believed that he was mentally ill. However, they failed to realize that he was a genius in the making, something his mother overlooked.

Things You Can Learn from Edison

There are many things that you can learn from Edison's life and how he lived. The man was a walking inspiration if you only knew where to look. There are things that you can learn from his life as well, and things you can learn from his inventions. This chapter is all about what you can learn from his life, and how you can apply it to your own.

This is what Edison did while he lived with his mentor for a while. He studied the man that he looked up to, and he learned about things that he could use to better himself. Things from the man's past that he overcome, to inspire Edison whenever he got discouraged. Ideas that the man was stumped on, Edison took and made better. Edison was constantly learning things to make his life better.

So what can you learn from him? Read below to find out.

Learn: It is never too late to learn something new. Edison was constantly learning new things, even as he got older. From the time he was a young boy to the time he died, he never lost his voracity for learning. If there was something new to read, he read it. If there was a new demonstration, he went to it. If one of his workers had learned something new, he wanted to know it as well. He was never satisfied with what he knew.

That is how you can learn from him. In today's age, a lot of people go to school, and listen to what they are taught, and take it at that. No one ever questions what they learned, or tries to go out and learn more on a subject that there was not much information on. There is only so much time that you are in school, yet there is so much to learn. You cannot possibly learn it all in those twelve short years that you spend in the four prison-like walls. Besides, school is supposed to teach you how to learn, if you don't use those skills outside of the classroom, what are you even showing up for. Challenge what you learn as well. Is it completely factually accurate, or is it a glossy representation because they feel the truth is too gruesome for you? Go to the library and check out a book on the subject you are challenging. In fact, check out several books on the subject. Make sure that some of them are biographies from the people that actually experienced it. Read them. Be like Edison, never be satisfied until you have read everything you possibly could about the subject. You will find that the more you know, the more you can understand other things that may not seem like they correlate with what you know.

Don't just learn from books, though. Learn from other people. Ask questions, hear their stories. Walk down your street. If you live in a more populated area, chances are you have seen a homeless person on the streets. Talk to one, or talk to many. They are people, and they have stories. If you think that they are criminals, or otherwise have an aversion to them, you will be surprised to learn about the circumstances that got them there in the first place. A lot of them are disabled veterans. Once you have learned about the hardships in life and learned about the people who would love what we all take for granted, you can move on to other people. A musician, or an artist. Someone in a line of work that you are interested in. Talk, ask questions, and truly listen to the answers you get. This is what Edison did. He learned from others almost as much as he learned from books. Be like Edison and never stop learning.

You can also learn from the workplace as well. Even if you are in a job where you think you could learn nothing. A lot of people view fast food jobs this way. However, that is the farthest from the truth. You can learn a lot from even the smallest of jobs. You can learn everything from how to leave your problems at the door, to real and valuable people skills. You will learn everything you need to know about the food you are making and will be able to apply that to your everyday life when you cook for yourself and others. You will also learn how to multitask.

How you can apply this to life:

Everything you learn, you can carry with you. You would be surprised when you might need to know something about an obscure fact you learned. Remembering things that might seem irrelevant can help you in your future because if you were ever in a tight situation, you could use your knowledge to help you figure out a solution. This is what Edison did. He learned about everything he could and used it in his experiments. A good motto to use is: When in doubt, learn it.

Persevere: Edison was the type of person who never gave up. If he couldn't figure something out, he would try until he finally got it right. He would try a million and one ways, and if those did not work, he would try a million and one more. Sure he got frustrated, but he kept going. He would spend long hours in his lab work, and he often did not sleep for more than a few hours a night until he got everything just right. His mind was constantly working, and eventually, he would get the right result.

In today's age, too many people give up if they can't get something right away. They try a new hobby and think that if they don't reach expert levels the first try that they are not good enough, and they just give up. This is the opposite of what you should do. Rome wasn't built in a day, and neither is a new skill. You have to keep trying until you reach the desired end result. Edison was a perfect embodiment of "practice makes perfect" and "if at first, you don't succeed, try, try again." This was because he never gave up, and you shouldn't either.

Say, for example, you are trying to cook a new dish. You get all of the ingredients together, and you put it in, and you cook it. You follow the directions to a 't' and still it doesn't come out tasting quite right. Do you throw in the towel, and say you are never making that dish again? No. You try it a different way. Sure the directions may say one thing, but sometimes you have to try things that may not seem obvious. Try adding a different seasoning, or cooking it for a little less time or a little more time. Make more mistakes, and learn what not to do. Eventually, that dish will be a favorite of the household. Keep trying, because that is the only way that you will succeed.

If you have tried any of the domestic housewife skills, whether you are a guy or a girl, chances are, it was not easy for you the first time. For example, crocheting. This is a hard skill to learn, and it takes a lot of patience and perseverance to get it right. You will not be able to whip up a pair of socks in two hours on your first try. First, you have to be proficient at making a simple pot holder or scarf and go from there. If you make a mistake, don't throw in the towel, try again. Keep trying until you have become good enough to make the thing that you want to make, and when you get good enough there, you can try something else, and it will get a lot easier to try higher level things.

How you can apply this to your life

As the above examples state, you can use these to succeed at new hobbies or even a new job. You just have to keep

Chapter 6: Another Relatable Inspiration - Thomas Edison

trying when you make a mistake. Remember, you do not fail, you merely find ways to do it wrong. That is a mantra that you should remember, as it is actually quite inspiring when you think about it. You made a mistake, so what, that is one more way not to do it, so keep going until you find the way to do it right.

Take risks: This is one of the most important things that Edison did. He caught fire in a boxcar due to one of these risks. Yet he kept on going with his risks and his experiments. Edison never lets a little danger, or discomfort stop him, and though there were some consequences, he kept on going taking even more risks. Whether they were physically or financially, he took them. I mean, the man was going to nearly double Tesla's salary[2]. That in itself was a big risk because he was a foreigner, and back then no one trusted foreigners.

A lot of people are scared to take risks, and they stay in the same rut that they are in, and complain that life is boring.

---

[2] Edison worked with a man named Nikola Tesla, who is referred to in the English language as simply, Tesla. When he hired Tesla, he paid him double his previous salary.

Some people take risks such as bungee jumping or skydiving, and they seem a lot happier, but thrill risks are not the only risks in life. Going for that big job you always wanted, even if it means moving to an entirely new area, asking a crush out on a date, buying a new car. All of these are risks that you could take, and it would bring so much more joy to life if you take them.

Think of something risky you would never do. Now think of the success you could have if you did take that risk. Money, fame, happiness? The riskiest things are generally the most rewarding. If you are not willing to quit your job to try to get the bigger one, maybe try just applying to the bigger one first, and keep your job that you are currently in. Just applying is a risk in itself, because you are putting yourself out there and getting your hopes up, and you might not get the job, which could be devastating. However, you cannot think about not getting it, as that would mess up the vibe, and you would be more than likely not get the job. You have to take the risk of the feeling that it is going to pay off.

You can also take a risk by investing money into a company to buy controlling interest. This is something that Edison did quite frequently. He would invest in a company, whether the company was destined to succeed or fail. If he liked the concept, he put his money on the line. Most of the time, with Edison's help, the company succeeded until he decided to sell off his stocks in the company, then they would either fail shortly thereafter or continue succeeding. Invest in something that is just starting up. Even if it is a small amount at first. The more you put yourself out there, the more reward you stand to receive. And that makes life more enjoyable, even if you don't get the gold, you still participated in the race, and that is what is fun in life. Trying new things and taking risks.

How you can apply this in your life

You don't have to jump off of tall buildings, or out of an airplane unless that is what you are into, but taking risks can fulfill areas in your life that you feel is lacking something. This makes life more colorful, and more enjoyable. Imagine what it would be like if you could wake up each day and look forward to the day ahead, even on Mondays. It is a nice thought, and it is possible if you start taking risks. Sure playing it safely keeps you from getting hurt, but half of the fun in life is the thrill of doing something that is not the safest thing to be doing. The thrill of failure, or the thrill of the risk of failure to be more precise.

Keep Moving: This is one thing that Edison did quite well. Whenever he invented something and got it to where it was the best that he thought he could get it, he moved on to something else. He did not spend his whole life on one invention, which is why he had over a thousand patents in his lifetime. He constantly kept moving on to new things, and tried to create as many things as he could, and would often have several projects going at once. While he did not give up until the invention was complete, he did not devote his life to that single invention until it was done, rather he would go work on something else, and often get an idea from another invention.

Chapter 6: Another Relatable Inspiration - Thomas Edison

Today's society is so caught up in the idea that you have to finish something before you can move on. Reading books, for instance, most people look down on those who read multiple books at one time and say that they person has an issue with commitment when in reality it is just boring to stay focused on one thing at a time. The best things in life come in pairs they always say, so why do we have to focus on only one thing at a time? If you are doing a job, you have to focus on the job you are doing. You are not allowed to be at work and check your stock market values at the same time. You have to wait until your workday is over, or until you get a break. If you are working on a project, you have to finish that project before you can move on to the next one. Especially in school. If you are doing a project for one lesson and you know what the project is going to be for the next lesson, you still have to finish the one you are on before going to the next thing. You can't finish both and turn them in at the same time because you will get reprimanded for not focusing enough on the task at hand.

This is a very limiting type of instruction. The mind is designed to multitask and handle multiple things at one time, and by training your mind to only handle one thing at a time, you are doing yourself a disservice, because there are times where you are going to have to do a few things at one time, and if you have trained your brain away from that, you will get overwhelmed. You have to keep your mind ready to multitask and to be able to take on multiple things at one time.

Just think back to the fast food example. You have to multitask to work in fast food, and if you are used to focusing on one task at a time, it can be exceedingly difficult, because often you have to take an order while serving someone else, and make sure that food is not burning, because most fast food restaurants are not known to be efficiently staffed, and are often way understaffed. You have to learn to focus on multiple things at the same time, rather than give things your undivided attention. This is something that Edison learned at an early age. He would often work on experiments while working at a job. Sometimes it caused problems, but that is the risk he was willing to take to become a great inventor.

How you can apply this to your life

Retrain your brain. You have to be able to multitask to become the person you want to be. Most high-level jobs, you generally only have to focus on one thing, but in lower level jobs, you have to focus on many. That is the problem with society though. They train you for the higher level jobs, not the lower level ones that you have to start at to make it to the top. So you have to retrain your mind yourself and make sure that you have sufficiently learned how to multitask.

You can also take this with you when you are learning new skills. You can learn multiple new skills at one time, rather than learning one and moving on to another, and so on and so forth. This saves time, as you can use things that you are learning in one skill to help you learn more about another skill, and this was Edison's way of thinking. Doing something on one invention could help him solve a problem on another invention. It can help you as well.

Encourage Others: Edison's mother encouraged him to be the best he could be, even though she had been told that he was addled. She worked really hard because she believed that in her son was a genius just waiting to be released. As told in the story in the above chapter, she did not tell Edison that he was mentally ill, and so he never knew. He believed that he could do anything.

In the same style, we should treat others. Rather than dragging them down, we should help them to believe that they are capable of doing whatever they set their minds too, regardless of disability. Just as we should encourage ourselves.

Anymore this world is so full of negativity. If someone comes home with a note from school saying his or her child is not fit for a normal classroom and instead needs special education because the teachers can't handle them, the parents don't pull the child out and homeschool them themselves, they let their child feel like they are not good enough to succeed, and plant that seed of doubt in their child's mind. If they see someone who is trying to do what they believe can't be done, they say that it is impossible and that the person should just give up. We also tear ourselves down. Whenever we think of doing something that is hard, our brains kick into saying that it is impossible, and it shouldn't even be attempted. We are our own self-destroyers, and we are very good at bringing ourselves down. This causes us to bring others down as well.

We need to get away from that trend, and back to encouraging people to be the best they can be. Edison didn't invent the lightbulb by saying that it is impossible, he invented it because people believed in him, and believed that it could be done. We have to build ourselves, and others up. If you see someone attempting something hard, encourage them, and see if there is anything you can do to help them achieve their goal, rather than telling them it can't be done, and then using the phrase "I care enough to not want them to get their hopes up, only to have them crushed." that is not caring. A good friend or family member does everything in their power to help that person succeed, not tell them to not even try, so they don't fail.

How you can apply this to your life

Encourage others: You never know when you might be the reason the succeed. You never know how much confidence you gave them, or how close they could have been to give up. Encourage yourself on something that you feel may be hard to do, rather than discouraging yourself to save yourself from failure, for not trying is the surest way to fail

As you can see, there are several things that you can learn from Edison, and how he lived his life. The man was constantly learning, and in that fashion, you should strive to be the same. The more you know, the more you can grow. The more knowledge you receive the father you can take yourself. And who knows, if you learn some things from other humans, you might find some new friends. People are very interesting, and there is much to learn from them. There is also much to learn from books as well, as books have a history just waiting to be unleashed. If you go to your library, there are millions of pages of knowledge sitting patiently, waiting to be read, and learned from. You can learn so much from the world, get out and explore it.

Chapter 6: Another Relatable Inspiration - Thomas Edison

You also can learn about taking risks from him. Not settling for the same old same old every day. Taking risks can bring a joy to your life that you probably didn't even realize was possible. You can also learn from taking a risk. You can learn what works for you and what does not work for you so that you can have that knowledge for when you try again and take the risk once more.

Which leads to perseverance. Edison was a firm believer in never giving up. He tried a million and one ways on every invention he ever created. He would work long hours and produce brilliant results, but just because he was a genius does not mean that he didn't have his struggles. The fluoroscope was one of those problems that he had. He had a hard time getting it quite right, and he suffered because of it, but he never gave up. After the fluoroscope was finished though, he never wanted to speak of it again due to the damage he sustained along with his assistant.

Encourage others to persevere as well, as Edison's mother did for him. The world is so full of other people trying to bring each other down; it doesn't need anymore. Be the one to build them up. Build yourself up as well. You never succeed when you don't even try. Be the one to push yourself to success.

And last but not least, Edison did not focus on anything for too long. He often jumped from task to task, starting one, and then another and jumping between them as he saw fit. If he got stumped on one, he would move to another and hoped that he could learn something from the new task to put towards the other task he was on. It is in the same fashion that we should try to take on multiple tasks rather than getting stuck on one, and not be able to move forward until it is done, creating a halt in productivity. Instead, we should have multiple tasks running so that we can always be working on something even if we get stumped on another task.

Conclusion

Thank you again for your purchase of this book. Hopefully, you found the information you needed to begin your journey to a happier mind. These tips are designed to expand your personal thinking skills by expanding your memory capabilities. It all ties into how your memory functions. If your memory does not function well, you will find that you may have problems with other areas of learning as well, as you can't access the information you so desperately need to.

If you liked the book, please take few minutes and **leave a review**. Thank you!

Click below link for your FREE book:

How Kindle Publishers from Non-authorized Countries Can Receive Royalties without the Wait or the Market Thresholds

http://receiveroyaltieswithoutthewait.gr8.com/

Or

Visit my author page to find more short guides:
https://goo.gl/4jB36A

Book 2

10 Interesting Facts About Your Own Mind that You Probably Don't Know

Ivan Harmon

Copyright 2017 by Ivan Harmon - All rights reserved.

The following book is reproduced with the goal of providing information that is as accurate and reliable as possible. Regardless, purchasing this ebook can be seen as consent to the fact that both the publisher and the author of this book are in no way experts on the topics discussed within and that any recommendations or suggestions that are made herein are for entertainment purposes only. Professionals should be consulted as needed prior to undertaking any of the action endorsed herein.

This declaration is deemed fair and valid by both the American Bar Association and the Committee of Publishers Association and is legally binding throughout the United States.

Furthermore, the transmission, duplication or reproduction of any of the following work including specific information will be considered an illegal act irrespective of if it is done electronically or in print. This extends to creating a secondary or tertiary copy of the work or a recorded copy and is only allowed with express written consent from the Publisher. All additional rights reserved.

The information in the following pages is broadly considered to be a truthful and accurate account of facts and as such any inattention, use or misuse of the information in question by the reader will render any resulting actions solely under their purview. There are no scenarios in which the publisher or the original author of this work can be in any fashion deemed liable for any hardship or damages that may befall them after undertaking information described herein.

Additionally, the information in the following pages is intended only for informational purposes and should thus be thought of as universal. As befitting its nature, it is presented without assurance regarding its prolonged validity or interim quality. Trademarks that are mentioned are done without written consent and can in no way be considered an endorsement from the trademark holder.

Table of contents

INTRODUCTION 1

1. WE CAN USE THREE TIMES MORE OF OUR BRAIN CAPACITY 3
2. YOU CAN TALK YOURSELF INTO BELIEVING IMPOSSIBLE THINGS 5
3. WHY IT'S DANGEROUS TO BE OVER-CONFIDENT 7
4. MULTI-TASKING AND SWITCHING CONTEXTS 9
5. WHY WE SEE PATTERNS WHERE THEY DON'T EXIST 11
6. STRESS CAN SHRINK YOUR BRAIN 15
7. MEDITATION REWIRES YOUR BRAIN FOR THE BETTER . 17
8. BEING TIRED IS GREAT FOR YOUR CREATIVITY 19
9. THE REASON WHY IT'S POSSIBLE TO BELIEVE ALMOST ANYTHING 21
10. HOW TO GET THE MOST USE OF YOUR MIND 23

CONCLUSION 27

Introduction

The exploration of the human mind is a journey of endless discoveries. Even with the progress science and psychology have made, we are still only scratching the surface of the profound and powerful capabilities, imagination and will hidden within the human brain.

The human psyche is full of mystery and complexity. No matter how much we think we know, there will always be more to learn and even more to understand. But, with every new breakthrough, we get a little closer to comprehension and being able to wrest more potential out of this amazing complexity of neurons and synapses.

Here are some amazing and surprising facts about the human mind that you probably don't now.

1. We Can Use Three Times More Of Our Brain Capacity

Early studies of the brain led us to believe that it's functional capacity was limited to 10%. This meant that of all our brain mass, only one tenth of it was actually used to perform functions. This widely accepted notion led people to believe that although we had the potential to use more of our brains, we hadn't yet unlocked that capability or that we had lost it over time. They thought that only one small portion of our brain was active and the rest remained dormant.

It turns out that this was totally wrong.

Scientific studies now show that various parts of our brains are activated and used at different times, based on the what we are doing, experiencing, or how we're exercising our minds (learning or remembering).

Sometimes the various parts of our brain activity even "overlap" each other, showing a combined use of different mental abilities to perform various functions.

In essence, this new idea means that humans might be capable of using up to 30% of our brain capacity at once.

Bottom line: *Don't underestimate the power of your brain!*

2. You Can Talk Yourself into Believing Impossible Things

We all know the world isn't exactly black and white. When it comes to morals, ethics and principles, however, there are always some things that will remain true. For example, we know lying and stealing are dishonest behaviors, just like we know courage and kindness are qualities of a good person.

People define themselves by the principles they practice, but at the same time, may find themselves committing acts that contradict these self-claimed ethics. For example, a person might consider themselves an honest person, but still lies or exaggerates.

How is this possible?

According to the Cognitive-Dissonance Theory, people can rationalize two opposing ideas to force them to make sense. This is a self-protective mechanism that we employ when we need to rationalize our questionable behaviors to fit better with our perceptions of ourselves. After all, no one likes to think they're a bad person. Instead, they come up with rationalizations for why they do bad things, but are still good people.

So, a liar can convince themselves that they're an honest person who tells "white" lies for good reasons.

Bottom line: *Your brain can make sense of almost anything in order to preserve our peace of mind and sense of self.*

3. Why it's dangerous to be over-confident

Speaking of effectiveness and productivity, there are countless people in the world that believe that they are highly effective and proficient at doing a lot of stuff. It's great to have a bit of confidence, but according to the Dunning-Kruger Effect, a lot of these people may be highly over-estimating their abilities.

Sometimes, people who are less-competent at a particular task may believe that they are great at it, or might convince others to believe so. This is because inexperienced people often underestimate the complexity of a new task.

When a person doesn't know enough about a job, they may assume that the process is simpler than it is and genuinely believe that they could perform it easily. This is essence of the Dunning-Kruger effect. Conversely, it also applies to highly competent people who underestimate their own abilities.

Bottom line: *Always assume there is more to know, rather than feeling like you know enough!*

4. Multi-Tasking and Switching Contexts

One of the ways we try to utilize that massive brain power is by multi-tasking. But in today's modern society, a lot of people are confusing traditional multi-tasking with context-switching.

What does this mean and why does it matter?

Multi-tasking is what we do when we're trying to perform several tasks simultaneously. Studies have found that this isn't always the best strategy when we're required to complete <u>different</u> activities to get the job done. The best approach to multi-tasking, according to the latest data, is to only work on multiple, <u>related</u> tasks. For example, working in the kitchen at a fast food restaurant. Even though a worker may be doing multiple tasks at once, all those tasks are related to achieving a main objective. That's when it works.

Context-Switching, however, is not the same at all. In fact, it's more likely to reduce our ability to complete a job correctly.

What is it?

It is when we try to do multiple tasks at once, but these tasks are unrelated. Imagine trying to watch TV, have a conversation with someone about politics, while trying to get some math homework done. That isn't multi-tasking, it's context-switching.

No matter how powerful your brain may be, it cannot effectively switch contexts without a loss of productivity as we focus and refocus on the varied and unrelated tasks. Even worse, switching contexts can even lower our IQ at performing certain tasks by up to 15 points.

Bottom line: *Multi-task at related tasks with the same underlying objective!*

5. Why We See Patterns Where They Don't Exist

Life is random, chaotic and nearly impossible to predict. But we, as humans, have a hard time accepting this reality. Maybe it's our egos, maybe it's our imaginations, but somehow, we want to believe that we can still control the unpredictability of life.

According to the Clustering Illusion, human beings attempt to discern clusters, patterns and rhythms in everything. (How many of us still look for events happening in clusters of 3?) That includes trying to discern order even in situations where there really is none, and where mathematical probability actually proves that it is not possible.

An example of this would be flipping a coin. The odds of flipping to either heads or tails is 50/50. Now, imagine an average human who is playing the odds of the coin toss in a gamble. That individual is inclined believe that if the coin showed tails 9 times out of 10, it should be heads on the tenth flip. Why? Because they are rationalizing that, "It's been tails for so long, it's bound to be heads the next time."

That is the basic human reaction to chaos. When trying to make sense of things, the individual is trying to discern some sort of cluster or pattern in an event that is solely determined by chance. But the law of probability doesn't change over time, and whether it's the first flip or the tenth, the odds remain exactly the same.

The same concept applies to regular life. People are constantly trying to determine patterns where there are none, in order to have a sense of control or the ability to predict what comes next.

Bottom line: *Life is chaotic. No matter how we try, we can't predict most of it, but we will still try to.*

6. Stress Can Shrink Your Brain

It may be a terrifying thought to realize that your brain might be shrinking. However, in a world full of excess stimuli, tight deadlines and uncontrollable changes – all sources of stress – you might be experiencing brain shrinkage.

Stress is the most common cause of changes in brain function, reducing our ability to function and perform to the best of our abilities. Even worse than that is the fact that stress actually causes your brain to shrink in size.

In fact, the areas related to stress in our brains may be enlarged to the detriment of our hippocampus, which actually shrinks in proportion. The hippocampus is the part of the brain that helps up form memories. The smaller our hippocampus is, the more prone to stress we become.

Bottom line: *Don't let stress get to you. Take a moment to breath and relax. Times change, and eventually so will the situations that stress you out.*

7. Meditation Rewires Your Brain for the Better

Did you know that you can rewire your brain to function better? Well, you can. This is possible through meditation.

Mediation has a lot of great benefits for your brain, body and overall health. One of the main benefits is that it helps us to deal with stress – avoiding the shrinking of our hippocampus. That's because meditation reduces anxiety.

Frequent mediation can loosen the connections of certain neural pathways, like those associated with ego and fear. It also strengthens bonds in other parts of our brain, like those associated with assessment and reasoning.

This can help us become more rational and less fearful people.

Meditation has other great effects too, like increasing our creativity and improving memory, among other things.

Bottom line: *Meditation can increase your brain functionality and make you a calmer, peaceful person.*

8. Being Tired is Great for Your Creativity

It is commonly believed that you need to be well-rested and wide awake to do your best creative work. However, that notion couldn't be further from the truth.

When it comes to analytical, task- and detail-oriented work, we do need a mind that is sharp and clear to do our best. However, when it comes to creative work and the application of imagination, we do better with a fuzzy brain.

Why?

When we're awake, our brain is alert and aware of rules and connections between known ideas and concepts. But when our brains are tired, we become less aware of these connections and often forget them altogether. As a result, our brains are forced to make new connections and be open to new concepts and ideas, therefore heightening our ability to be creative and come up with fresh thoughts.

In other words, when we're tired, our imaginations kick in and we start making stuff up rather than wondering what's realistic. In the end, we find ourselves arriving at new ways of thinking, resulting in some of our best creative work.

Bottom line: *Creative work can be done even when you're tired after work.*

9. The Reason Why It's Possible to Believe Almost Anything

The human mind is an amazing thing. It allows us to perceive and experience the world as we want to, rather than as it is. This has a lot to do with the fact that our subconscious mind is not capable of discerning between what is real and what our mind imagines.

We can create events and interactions, and then convince ourselves they were real. This is how false memories are formed. The decisive factor is how much emotion is associated with an event in our minds, whether real or fake, the more emotion, the more the subconscious believes it. As a result, we can trick our brains into believing almost anything!

Bottom line: *Be careful of what you imagine to be real; it is all real to the subconscious mind!*

10. How to Get the Most Use of Your Mind

Speaking of the subconscious mind, it can do a lot more than just confuse fantasy with reality. Our subconscious mind is the most powerful part of our brains. Without it, we wouldn't even be alive.

Our subconscious mind handles all the processes that keep our bodies functioning. Blinking, breathing, heart pumping, blood flowing, food digesting, bowel functioning, etc., are all handled by the subconscious mind. That's why we're not conscious of doing these things.

It's even in control when it comes to our reflex actions, like swatting a fly or moving out of the way when something is hurtling towards you. These are functions that our subconscious handles.

With a little practice and effort, we can program our subconscious mind to do just about anything.

An example of this is reading this right now. It's hard to imagine, but there once was a time when you had to fight to recognize and read each word. That was back when you were learning to read with your conscious mind. As you practiced reading consciously, you eventually handed the task over to your subconscious by programming the words and reading habits into your brain.

Now, when you read, your subconscious mind is doing most of the work, from recognizing the words to understanding the message being delivered by each sentence.

Likewise, you can train your mind to do a lot of stuff. First, you can believe in almost anything. Secondly, you can make – or break – any habit you want.

Bottom line: *If you learn to utilize the power of your subconscious mind, through habits like meditating, you can have all the power you'll ever need to be great at what you want to be.*

Conclusion

Perhaps one of the only certainties about the brain is how little we still know about it. Within that few pounds of grey matter exists a galaxy of possibilities and untrodden paths. As time passes and we learn more about how the brain works and what we're capable of, even more mysteries and wonders will be uncovered, leading to greater discoveries and expansion of our potential.

A little request from the author. Book reviews help to spread the good news about valuable information that is hidden behind the cover of a book. So if you found this book useful in any way, **a review** on Amazon is always appreciated. Thank you!

Book 3

10 Fun Facts About Your Memory

How Does Your Memory Work

Ivan Harmon

Copyright 2017 by Ivan Harmon - All rights reserved.

The following book is reproduced with the goal of providing information that is as accurate and reliable as possible. Regardless, purchasing this ebook can be seen as consent to the fact that both the publisher and the author of this book are in no way experts on the topics discussed within and that any recommendations or suggestions that are made herein are for entertainment purposes only. Professionals should be consulted as needed prior to undertaking any of the action endorsed herein.

This declaration is deemed fair and valid by both the American Bar Association and the Committee of Publishers Association and is legally binding throughout the United States.

Furthermore, the transmission, duplication or reproduction of any of the following work including specific information will be considered an illegal act irrespective of if it is done electronically or in print. This extends to creating a secondary or tertiary copy of the work or a recorded copy and is only allowed with express written consent from the Publisher. All additional rights reserved.

The information in the following pages is broadly considered to be a truthful and accurate account of facts and as such any inattention, use or misuse of the information in question by the reader will render any resulting actions solely under their purview. There are no scenarios in which the publisher or the original author of this work can be in any fashion deemed liable for any hardship or damages that may befall them after undertaking information described herein.

Additionally, the information in the following pages is intended only for informational purposes and should thus be thought of as universal. As befitting its nature, it is presented without assurance regarding its prolonged validity or interim quality. Trademarks that are mentioned are done without written consent and can in no way be considered an endorsement from the trademark holder.

Table of contents

INTRODUCTION 1

1. THE DOORWAY EFFECT 3

2. SCENT AND MEMORY 5

3. ALL-NIGHTERS: BENEFICIAL FOR STUDYING? 9

4. ALWAYS FORGETTING DREAMS? 13

5. SPAN MEMORY 15

6. DÉJÀ VU 17

7. MUSIC REALLY HELPS MEMORY 19

8. ENVIRONMENTAL IMPACT 21

9. STRESS AND MEMORY 23

10. EARLY MEMORIES 27

CONCLUSION 31

CHECK OUT OTHER BOOKS 33

Introduction

Congratulations on downloading your personal copy of *10 Fun Facts About Your Memory: How Does Your Memory Work.* Thank you for doing so.

Have you ever been at work and walked into your coworker's office only to realize you've completely forgotten the reason you were going in there? Do you wonder why you forget awesome dreams so quickly, or why a certain smell can trigger such a powerful memory?

The human brain is an amazing thing, and our ability to remember everything from the big, life-changing events that rock our world to the smallest details is complicated and fascinating.

Read on to learn some interesting facts about your memory and your brain, and find answers to some of the questions you've been wondering about, like whether you should pull that all-nighter or not

1. The Doorway Effect

We are all familiar with the situation. You are busy doing something, whether that's cleaning the house, doing paperwork at the office, or working on an arts and crafts project with the kids. You realize halfway through that you need something from the other room; you need to speak with your colleague about a document she gave you, the cleaning chemical you need is under the bathroom sink, or you left the construction paper in the other room. You get up to go retrieve whatever it was that you remembered, and get to your destination only to find that you've completely forgotten the reason you went there in the first place.

This is the Doorway Effect. It is a quirk of your short-term memory, and researchers say that the doorway itself could actually be to blame for this little failure. Psychologists say that the brain may view the doorway as a marker that a new scene is beginning, and that it should file the information from the other room away to prepare for new information. Going through a doorway is seen as an "event boundary", which signals to the brain that you are in a new situation now, and it compartmentalizes the old information and the new information. This compartmentalization makes it hard to remember what you entered the room for, as you are trying to access a memory that has been stored.

2. Scent and Memory

You've probably experienced the phenomenon of being in an unfamiliar place and smelling something that somehow seems familiar, and suddenly having memories rushing in about a certain place. Maybe you smell gardenias and are immediately mentally transported back to your grandmother's back yard, or the scent of hot asphalt takes you back to being a kid at amusement parks in the middle of summer.

The reason certain smells can bring back vivid memories is that your olfactory nerve is very close to the area of your brain that processes emotional memory. The amygdala is responsible for all those memories that are related to your feelings, whether good ones or bad ones. When you remember feeling super excited at the prospect of riding the big roller coaster for the first time, when you remember feeling sad about missing your grandmother, those memories are being processed by the amygdala.

Your olfactory nerve is also located close to your hippocampus, which is responsible for processing memory in general. With this nerve being so close to two major memory centers, it is no wonder your sense of smell is so closely tied to your memory. There has even been research that shows that when people sustain injuries to the parts of the brain that process memory, they experience impairment of their sense of smell, because in order for you to identify what you are smelling, you have to be able to remember the last place you smelled it.

Studies have even shown that if you study something while in the presence of a smell, you'll actually remember that information more vividly and intensely the next time you get a whiff of the smell than if you were just recalling the memory on your own.

3. All-Nighters: Beneficial for Studying?

Some people are great students. They take meticulous notes during classes, and dedicate time to spend reviewing them and committing them to memory well before they're tested on the information they learned. However, some people are not so organized, or they procrastinate and put off their studying, and find themselves scrambling to absorb and retain information in a short period of time before the test.

If you have ever been in that situation, you have probably experienced how cramming for a test last minute seems to only work sometimes. Some nights you can pull an all-nighter and be able to rattle off the information the next day, and sometimes it seems like everything you read immediately leaked out of your ears and is gone forever.

There is a reason for this. Your ability to retain information and remember it is related to sleep, and the type of thing you are trying to remember. Sleep is very important for what is called "procedural memory", and less important for what is termed "declarative memory". Basically, procedural memories are about how to do things, explanations and theories, memories that involve perceptual skills and motor skills. Declarative memories are more related to facts and being able to memorize them, without much of an explanation about them, like dates, or the Periodic Table of Elements.

So, in order to make the most of your studying and sleep, make sure you are aware of what type of memory you are dealing with. If you have a test the next day about the differences between the economics or the United States and France, you'd be better off getting a good night's rest, so your brain can recall that information better. However, if you are faced with a test where you have to list all of the irregular verb conjugations in Spanish, an all-nighter could actually benefit you.

4. Always Forgetting Dreams?

You have no doubt heard that people are constantly dreaming throughout the night and just can't remember those dreams. It can certainly be frustrating to wake up after a particularly strange fantasy only to forget it as soon as you go to tell your friend, but the reason for this occurrence is quite interesting.

When we sleep, our long-term memory shuts down temporarily, which is why we don't remember most of our dreams and dreams we had shortly before waking up usually fade quickly unless we write them down. This is also why, if someone wakes up for just a moment in the middle of the night, they may not remember waking up or what happened at all.

One thing you can do to try and remember some of those dreams is keep a little notebook beside your bed and write everything you remember down as quickly as possible. It is impossible to know how long you have before the thought disappears, but the quicker you write it down, the more you'll have saved from the recycle bin of your brain. This could even help you dream of it next time, if you go to sleep thinking about it.

So next time you dream up the perfect holiday or that treat-filled world all to yourself, jot it down as soon as you wake up, and you might just get lucky and dream about it some more.

5. Span Memory

On the subject of short term versus long-term memory, short-term memory isn't just limited by time! Our brains have a very finite amount of short-term memory. Specifically, most people can only store seven things in short-term memory at a time. This is why seven digits works well for phone numbers: on average, most people will be able to remember that, but not any more than that. If someone really wants you to call, they had better not give too much more information than that, or most people will start to forget the numbers.

The measure of checking your short-term memory is called your memory span. You can check out how your own short-term memory holds up by taking a memory span test online. Build up from 5 different numbers, letters, or words, to 6, then 7, and see if you can go any higher than that. There is another challenging test you can do as well - do the same, but remember them in reverse order. Tests for memory span contribute to some cognitive ability tests, to help work out how well somebody would do at taking notes from one meeting or glance at work. Store this one in your long-term memory: if you have to remember more than seven things, write them down!

6. Déjà Vu

Most of us are familiar with the term 'déjà vu'. That odd little feeling when you are in a situation that feels very familiar, or you feel like you've lived through that conversation already. There are different 'déjà experiences', such as 'déjà visité' and 'déjà vecu', but we usually lump it under the same term. Déjà visité is when you feel like you've visited a particular spot before, even if you've never been in that museum or that house until just then. Déjà vecu on the other hand is when you feel like you've already lived through something, such as that conversation about recent events, despite nothing like that happening before.

We are not quite sure why this happens, though there are lots of theories. Some people think that it might be related to source memory, which is the type of memory associated with when/where you learned particular information. Others think it has to do with the temporal lobe, which houses the hippocampus and helps form long-term memory. It could even be a bit of wish fulfillment, or a hiccup in the brain mistaking the present for the past. Whatever the cause, the majority of the population experiences it at some point.

7. Music Really Helps Memory

We have all had that one teacher who tries to help us remember pointless facts that we don't really need for our lives by putting it into song. Whether it was the US Presidents or the quadratic formula, sure enough, they stuck around. It is definitely easier to remember things with a tune, but that's not the only way music can help our memories. A study in Hong Kong by Dr. Agnes Chan found that even if what you are trying to remember is not musical, if you've studied music, your verbal memory will be more receptive and more lasting.

This isn't the first study to have similar findings, and the results are there: the longer you have studied music, the better your memory will be. Studying music will help activate the part of the brain that processes what you hear, allowing it to grow stronger and make more connections, ensuring that your auditory memory gets even better. So, if your family is always telling you that you don't remember anything they say, it might be worth picking up a guitar to train your brain!

Sometimes, people also find that they remember lyrics more than schoolwork, and songs made for learning can really help you learn more.

Think of tunes like the Alphabet Song, where you sing through each letter of the alphabet - have you got that out of your head yet? Catchy tunes like that can help firmly put the knowledge in your long-term memory, so find some more and keep on learning.

8. Environmental Impact

Everyone has had one of those days where you need to remember something and it just won't come to mind. Too often, this happens to us during a time when it is necessary that we remember the information, like during a test. No matter how hard you try, you just can't bring the information to mind. There are some theories about your environment's role on your memory retention that could help explain this problem.

Studies have come up with all sorts of interesting information about environment and memory retention. It is believed that you are better able to remember something if you are tested on it in the same type of environment you were in when you learned it. For example, if you studied and memorized the names of all of Henry VIII's wives in a quiet environment, you are more likely to be able to put them down on your test in a quiet room than you would be if you were tested on them in a noisier environment. By the same note, if you learned a mathematical formula during a rambunctious study session with friends, it is going to be more difficult for you to rattle off that formula in a quiet classroom.

However, your environment will impact different types of memory differently. Quiet or loud environments are more likely to affect your ability to recall information that requires you to bring up memories and interpret information into your own words, like essays. Learning and testing environments are less likely to affect your ability to recognize information, though, like on multiple-choice tests.

So, the next time you are studying for a test you know is going to take place in a silent room, try studying in a similar environment. If you know you'll hear background noise during your test, try one of those websites that provide background noise. You may be surprised how much more you remember!

9. Stress and Memory

On the subject of testing, here is another likely familiar scenario: you are taking a class you are fairly confident in. You perform well during lectures, your homework comes back to you with good grades, and your papers are well thought out and concise. You are not worried. . . until something goes wrong in your personal life.

Maybe you broke things off with your significant other, you got bad news about a family member, or you are having financial troubles. Your exam is coming up and you are studying like crazy, all the while with this stress in your mind. You find it harder and harder to focus on what you are studying, which increases your stress levels, and when it comes time to take the exam, you find that you can't remember the information you studied. Older information is there, but nothing recent, and nothing on the exam.

The problem isn't that you can't remember the information. The problem is that you didn't memorize it properly to begin with. Memory is actually a process with three steps: encoding, consolidation, and retrieval. Most of us only think about the retrieval part when we think of memory; the ability to recall the information is what's important, right? Not so. The more important aspects of your memory are the encoding and consolidation steps. They're the steps that make it possible for you to recall the information later.

Think of it as creating a text document on your computer. First you have to write the words: this is the encoding step. Next you have to save it. That's consolidation. Finally, you are able to pull up that document later and reference it. That's retrieval. When you encode the information, you pull it from your environment, for example, a textbook. When you consolidate it, you are moving it from your short-term memory into your long-term memory.

In order to be able to remember it down the line, it has to make it to your long-term memory. If something gets in the way of that, like stress, consolidation doesn't happen, and you are unable to retrieve the memories when you need them. Stress acts as an interference between the encoding and consolidation steps.

So, it is not that you didn't remember your doctor's appointment, it is that you got a stressful phone call right after you made the appointment, so the information didn't make it to your long-term memory in the first place.

10. Early Memories

Before you turned five years old, you accomplished a lot. You walked for the first time, said your first words, ate your first foods (and probably discovered which foods you loved and that you hated spinach), discovered all sorts of new places and made all kinds of friends. You had a lot of experiences as a tiny human, and chances are, you remember almost none of them. If you try to think back and remember your first taste of ice cream, or the day you met your first puppy, you likely either come up blank or remember something that may or may not be a memory of a story someone else told you about your childhood, rather than a genuine memory you have yourself.

For a long time, scientists thought that the reason we have so few memories from our childhood was that babies just didn't retain information in that way. They didn't make memories. Some thought that children were making memories, but lacked the ability to communicate and verbalize them. The most recent research, however, has suggested that we begin making memories from the time we are in the womb, and we are perfectly capable of recalling and verbalizing them as soon as we are able to talk.

The reason you can't remember most of your childhood has now been chalked up to what's called infant or childhood amnesia. it is believed that because we are basically sponges for information as children, we take on so much that our brains just can't remember all of it.

To make room for new information and more important memories that will affect our lives in a more profound way, the brain deletes most of what it absorbed during the early years. This increases the older we get. At 3 years old, a child is able to recount most of what they have experienced, but if you ask that child to recount the same experiences again at 7 years old, and then again at 12, you'll see a rapid decrease in the amount they are able to remember.

So, parents, if you want your kids to be able to remember their first birthday party later in their lives, be sure to write it all down so you can help fill in the blanks!

Conclusion

Thank for making it through to the end of *10 Fun Facts About Your Memory: How Does Your Memory Work.* Let's hope it was informative and able to provide you with all of the tools you need to achieve your goals of maximizing your memorization abilities and learning about your brain!

If you found this book useful in any way, **a review** on Amazon is always appreciated. Thank you!

Please visit my author page at **https://goo.gl/LcR8wD** to find more other books about *memory*.

Check Out Other Books

Please go here to check out other books that might interest you:

Memory Exercises: Create a habit for memory enhancement by Ivan Harmon

What Your Boss Never Wants You to Know: How to Find Your Strengths, Work Happier, Grow Your Expertise, and Rediscover Your Life
by Lam Thanh Hue

Dr. How's series

Printed in Great Britain
by Amazon